THE TRINITY

DISCOVERING THE DEPTH OF THE NATURE OF GOD

CHARLES R. SWINDOLL

WITH STUDY HELPS BY VAL HARVEY

BROADMAN
& HOLMAN
PUBLISHERS

Nashville, Tennessee

© 1986 by Charles R. Swindoll, Inc.
Originally published by Multnomah Press
Portland, Oregon 97266
Study questions © 1993 by Broadman Press,
1997 by Broadman & Holman Publishers
Nashville, Tennessee 37234

ISBN: 0-8054-0162-8

Dewey Decimal Classification: 236
Subject Heading: TRINITY

Printed in the United States of America

Scripture quotations, unless otherwise marked, are from the NASB, the New American Standard Bible, © the Lockman Foundation, 1960, 1962, 1963, 1968, 1971, 1972, 1973, 1975, 1977; used by permission.

Scripture references marked NIV are from the Holy Bible, New International Version, copyright © 1973, 1978, 1984 by International Bible Society.

Scripture references marked TLB are from The Living Bible, copyright © Tyndale House Publishers, Wheaton, Ill., 1971, used by permission.

Scripture references marked AMP are from The Amplified Bible, Old Testament copyright © 1962, 1964 by Zondervan Publishing House, used by permission, and the New Testament © The Lockman Foundation 1954, 1958, 1987, used by permission.

Scripture references marked GNB are from the Good News Bible, the Bible in Today's English Version. Old Testament: Copyright © American Bible Society 1976; New Testament: Copyright © American Bible Society 1966, 1971, 1976. Used by permission.

Scripture references marked Phillips are reprinted with permission of Macmillan Publishing Co., Inc. from J. B. Phillips: The New Testament in Modern English, revised edition, © J. B. Phillips 1958, 1960, 1972.

Scripture references marked KJV are from the King James Version of the Bible.

Scripture references marked MLB are from The Modern Language Bible, The New Berkeley Version. Copyright 1945, 1959 © 1969 by Zondervan Publishing House. Used by permission.

THE TRINITY

This volume is affectionately
dedicated to four faithful men:

_____

Cyril Barber
Bill Butterworth
David Lien
Bill Watkins

_____

who serve behind the scenes at Insight
for Living, giving counsel and
encouragement to those who hurt,
finding in Scripture the foundation of
their faith. I am indebted to each man
for his unswerving commitment to
God's truth, his unselfish ministry to
people in need, his unceasing
discipline to stay at an endless task,
and his unsurpassed loyalty to my wife
and me as friends.

Contents

Introduction 9

Part 1: God the Father. 19

  1. Knowing God: Life's Major Pursuit. 21

  2. The Wail of a Weeping Prophet. 27

  3. The Importance of Knowing God. 33

  4. Finally, Some Essential Facts. 43

  5. Loving God: Our Ultimate Response. 47

  6. God of Grace, God of Mercy 54

  7. Man of Gratitude, Man of Love 62

  8. For Those Who Truly Love God. 66

Part II: The Lord Jesus Christ 69

  9. Mary's Little Lamb 71

10. The Background Behind Jesus' Birth. 76

11. The Scene in Bethlehem 82

12. Mary's Lamb. 86

13. The Significance of the Insignificant 90

14. When the God-Man Walked Among Us. 93

15. Examples of Humanity and Deity. 106

16. Changing Lives Is Jesus' Business. 114

17. Three Lives Jesus Changed. 124

Part III: The Holy Spirit. 143

18. The Spirit Who Is Not a Ghost. 145

19. Some Things the Holy Spirit Is Not 151

20. Some Reasons the Holy Spirit Is Here. 158

21. Some Ways the Holy Spirit Is Felt 168

Notes 173

Introduction

For years I have wanted to write on doctrine . . . Bible doctrine. My flesh has been willing, but my spirit has been weak. That calls for an explanation.

The need for knowledge of the Scripture is obvious. Everywhere I turn I meet or hear about well-meaning Christians who are long on zeal but short on facts . . . lots of enthusiasm and motivation but foggy when it comes to scriptural truth.

They have a deep and genuine desire to be used by God, to reach the lost, to serve in the church, to invest their energies in "the kingdom of God and His righteousness," but their doctrinal foundation is shifting sand rather than solid rock. The result is predictable: They are at the mercy of their emotions, flying high one day and scraping the bottom the next. A frustrating yo-yo syndrome.

I know. For more years than I care to remember, I, too, climbed and tumbled, soared, and submerged, thought I knew the scoop, then later discovered how off-target I really was. The whole miserable mess leaves a person filled with doubt and disillusionment, grossly lacking in confidence, not to mention having that awful feeling of being exposed. At that point, most Christians decide to pack it in lest they get caught again in a similar position of vulnerability. You and I may be amazed to know how many have retreated into the background scenery of passivity simply because their ignorance of the basic building blocks caused them embarrassment.

Like I said, the need is obvious. Being a fixer-upper type, I am prompted to jump in with both feet and crank out a pile of pages that will provide the doctrinal ammunition so many Christians need. That's why I said my flesh is willing. But since I am also a let's-be-realistic type, I am reluctant.

Among the last things believers need is another dull volume on doctrine. Sterile and unapplied theology interests no one living in the real world. Most of those books wind up as great (and expensive!) doorstops. They also make a good impression when the pastor drops by for a visit and sees them lying there, freshly dusted, on the coffee table. And there is nothing like wading through thick theological works late at night to cure your battle with insomnia. Who hasn't come close to fracturing his nose on an eight-pound volume while trying to make it past page 3 in the prone position?

That's why my spirit is weak. Deep within me has been this growing fear of just pumping out another thick, boring book on doctrine that looks good but reads bad.

Theology Needs to Be Interesting

Since I am committed to accuracy, clarity, and practicality, I loathe the thought of publishing something that is anything but interesting, easily understood, creative—and yes, even captivating. See why my desire to write a book on doctrine has been on the back burner so long? It isn't easy to communicate the deepest truths of the Bible in an interesting manner. It has taken years for me to be convinced that it can be done . . . and even more years to be convinced that I may be able to do it. The chapters that follow are my best effort at accomplishing this objective. Only time will tell whether I have achieved my desire.

If my stuff makes sense, if the average individual is able to follow my thinking, picture the scenes, grasp my logic, come to similar conclusions, and later pass on a few of those thoughts to someone else, then the book will have made the impact I desired. But if it lacks real substance, or if the reader discovers it requires a graduate degree to track my thoughts, or even if it proves to be true to the biblical text yet comes across as tedious and pedantic, then my face, I can assure you, will be as red as your nose.

Introduction

The Need to Improve Theology's Reputation

Frankly, theology has gotten a bum rap. Just ask around. Make up a few questions and try them on for size in your church. You'll see. Many folks, if they are candid with you, will confess a distaste for sound biblical doctrines. Sound theology, like Rodney Dangerfield, "don't get no respect." You question that? Then let me suggest you do your own personal survey among some Christians. Ask things like:

- Ever made a study of the doctrines in the Bible?
- How would you respond if your pastor announced plans to bring a series of pulpit messages on several "important theological subjects"?
- Do you believe that all Christians ought to know where they stand doctrinally, or is that more the business of the clergy?
- When you hear the word *theology*, do you have a mental image of something interesting and stimulating? Or do you honestly think, *Dull stuff . . . please don't bore me?*
- On a scale of one to ten (ten being most important), how high would you rate a knowledge of theology?
- Can you remember a doctrinal sermon—or one lesson on theology you were involved in—that you actually *enjoyed*?
- Choosing your preference, rearrange these topics in the order you consider most interesting and timely. Which interests you the most? The least? Give each a number from one to seven.
  - _____ a biographical look at a biblical character
  - _____ a verse-by-verse analysis of a book in the New Testament
  - _____ a serious study of biblical doctrines
  - _____ what God's Word teaches about the home and family
  - _____ moral, social, and ethical issues according to Scripture
  - _____ biblical principles for success and personal motivation

———— Proverbs made practical for today

Unless you are most unusual, the study of doctrine would be ranked toward the bottom, if not altogether in last place. Compared to success principles on the home and family, "a serious study of biblical doctrines" does not seem nearly as important or relevant to most evangelical congregations. Yet, believe it or not, at the very heart of all those other topics is a great deal of theology.

It is surprising for most Christians to hear that their doctrinal position determines their interpretation and application of Scripture—whether or not they have ever declared themselves doctrinally. What roots are to a tree, the doctrines are to the Christian. From them we draw our emotional stability, our mental food for growth, as well as our spiritual energy and perspective on life itself. By returning to our roots, we determine precisely where we stand. We equip ourselves for living the life God designed for us to live.

Why Is Doctrine Often So Dull?

If all this is true, then why does the mere mention of theology turn off so many people? Why are most churches full of people programmed to think that doctrine is a synonym for dullness and boredom?

At the risk of appearing ultracritical, I'll be frank with you. Much of the problem lies with theologians who have done a poor job of communicating their subject. No offense, theological scholars, but you are notorious for talking only to yourselves. The language you employ is clergy code-talk, woefully lacking in relevance and reality. The terms you use are in-house jargon, seldom broken down into manageable units for people who aren't clued in. You may be accurate and certainly sincere, but your world is like the television series of yesteryear, "One Step Beyond." Please understand that we love you and respect you. No one would dare to question your brilliance. We need your gifts in the body and we admire your ability to stay at the disciplines of your studies. We just don't understand you.

As a result, much of what you write is kept within those

cloistered chambers that intimidate people who haven't had the privilege of probing the heavenlies as you have. The majority feel a distance from you when you share your secrets. I realize that many of you wish this weren't so, but I suppose it comes with the territory.

In this book and the others in this study series, my hope is to build a bridge of theological understanding with the common man, the uninitiated individual, the person who has never been to seminary—and doesn't care to to go—but really does want to develop a solid network of doctrinal roots.

I'm interested in reaching the truck driver, the athlete, the waitress, the high school student, the person in the military service, the homemaker who has a houseful of kids at her feet, the business person whose world is practical, earthy, tough, and relentless . . . and a hundred other "types" who have the brains to absorb biblical truth but lack the time and patience to look up every sixth or seventh word in a dictionary.

I therefore make no apology for approaching various subjects in a different way than standard theologians. I want everyone who picks up this book to understand every word and grasp every principle, even if you don't agree with them. (To disagree with me is your privilege—I expect it. In fact, I invite it. But to misunderstand or to *fail* to understand what I'm getting at would be tragic.)

I freely confess that I want you to enjoy this journey . . . to find out that discovering doctrine and seeing its importance can encourage you like nothing else. I want us to laugh together, as well as think together, as we dig into *the Book*. It's been my observation for the past twenty-five years of ministry that there is no subject too deep for anyone to understand if the material is presented creatively and clearly, sparked periodically by humor, and accompanied by illustrations that let plenty of life in. All this is true of folks who really want to learn.

By the way, that brings up another reason doctrine is dull to some people. As I implied earlier, they have a built-in, long-standing *prejudice* against it. Somehow, they have convinced themselves that (a) they don't need to fuss around with heady stuff like that since they aren't doing "full-time ministry," or (b) even if they made a study of the doctrines, all that knowledge would be of little practical value. In subtle ways these two excuses tend to plug their ears and clog the learning process.

Without trying to perform an overkill, both of those excuses are totally erroneous. Because every Christian is "doing full-time ministry," being theologically informed and equipped could not be more important. And since when does a knowledge of important facts lack practical value? If I recall Jesus' words correctly, that which makes us free is knowing the truth. It's ignorance that binds us, not knowledge. Furthermore, we are left defenseless before the cults and other persuasive false teachers if we lack this solid network of doctrinal roots. As I stated earlier, it stabilizes us.

An Approach that Will Keep Things Interesting

Before we get underway, let me explain my plan of approach.

I have no intention of writing an exhaustive theological treatment on all the biblical doctrines. (If you happen to be a perfectionist, expecting every jot and tittle to be addressed in this volume or the others in this series, please read that sentence again.) My plan is to offer a broad-brush approach to most of the essential points of evangelical truth. If you find certain details are not covered to your satisfaction or if you observe that some subjects of interest to you are not even mentioned, just remember that is on purpose. I'm hoping to whet your appetite for a much more intense and thorough study *on your own* once you've begun to get excited about these essential areas. Who knows? Maybe one day *you'll* be the one who will write a more thorough and analytical work. Be my guest.

You'll also want to keep a Bible handy. I'll try to quote as many of the main verses and passages as possible. But there will be times that I will give an additional reference or two which you might want to look up right then. If you have the time, please do that. Before too long you will begin to feel much more at home in the Scriptures. And use a good study Bible rather than a loose paraphrase or a copy of just the New Testament.

There are a number of study tools that make the Bible and its people come to life for you. *Commentaries* explore books of the Bible and tell you what scholars have discovered about the writers of the books, the times in which they lived, and what the Scriptures mean. *Bible encyclopedias, dictionaries,* and *handbooks* contain information about the people, places, and events in the Bible. They often include drawings and pictures to help you put yourself in the first-century world. *Bible atlases* have maps that show how the Holy Land looked at various times throughout history. Atlases usually give background information about governments and geography. *Concordances* tell you where words appear in the Bible. Pick a word like *love*; look it up just like you would in a dictionary; and you'll find a list of verses in which *love* is used. If you're serious about Bible study, you'll want to stop by a bookstore and invest in a good Bible handbook, atlas, and concordance. You'll be surprised how much those resources will add to your study.

At the end of the first chapter of each part of this book you will note several thoughts I call "Root Issues." These are simply practical suggestions designed to help you keep the doctrines out of the realm of sterile theory and in touch with the real world. To get the most out of these, I'd recommend that you purchase a handy-sized spiral notebook—your personal "Root Issues Notebook"—to record your thoughts, observations, and responses. Each chapter concludes with study questions. "Extending Your Roots" helps you explore what we've been talking about. "Taproot" takes you even further in your study of each doctrine. Don't be afraid to write your answers in this book. It's yours—make it personal.

Ten Major Areas of Doctrine

Finally, the outline I want to follow will be interwoven in this series of five study guides. All the doctrines I want to cover will fall within these ten major categories:

- The Bible
- God the Father
- The Lord Jesus Christ
- The Holy Spirit
- The Depravity of Humanity
- Salvation
- The Return of Christ
- Resurrection
- The Body of Christ
- The Family of God

As I mentioned earlier, the list is purposely not exhaustive, but there is plenty here to get our roots firmly in place. In fact, the better-known historic creeds down through the ages have included these ten areas. While considering this recently, I decided to write my own doctrinal credo, a statement of my personal faith. What it may lack in theological sophistication I have tried to make up for in practical terminology.

As I return to the roots of my faith, I am encouraged to find the time-honored foundations firmly intact:

- I affirm my confidence in God's inerrant Word. I treasure its truths and I respect its reproofs.
- I acknowledge the Creator-God as my Heavenly Father, infinitely perfect, and intimately acquainted with all my ways.
- I claim Jesus Christ as my Lord—very God who came in human flesh—the object of my worship and the subject of my praise.
- I recognize the Holy Spirit as the third member of the Godhead, incessantly at work convicting, convincing, and comforting.
- I confess that Adam's fall into sin left humanity without the hope of heaven apart from a new birth, made possible by the Savior's death and bodily resurrection.
- I believe the offer of salvation is God's love-gift to all. Those who accept it by faith, apart from works, become new creatures in Christ.

Introduction

- I anticipate my Lord's promised return, which could occur at any moment.
- I am convinced that all who have died will be brought back from beyond—believers to everlasting communion with God and unbelievers to everlasting separation from God.
- I know the Lord is continuing to enlarge His family, the universal body of Christ, over which He rules as Head.
- I am grateful to be a part of a local church which exists to proclaim God's truth, to administer the ordinances, to stimulate growth toward maturity, and to bring glory to God.

With confidence and joy, I declare this to be a statement of the essentials of my faith.

That's where I stand . . . sort of a preview of coming attractions. Now it's time for you to dig in and discover where you stand. With God's help I think you will find this study one of the most important and interesting projects you have ever undertaken. You may even get so "fanatical" about your faith that your whole perspective on life changes.

Come to think of it, that's exactly what Christianity is supposed to do . . . change our lives.

I wish to thank my long-term, splendid secretary as I have so many times before. Helen Peters has done it again. Without regard for her own needs and preferences, she has deciphered my hand scratching, typed and retyped my manuscript, verified my footnotes, corrected my spelling, and helped me meet my deadlines. "Thank you" seems hardly sufficient to declare the depth of my gratitude. I also want to thank Val Harvey for her excellent work in writing the study questions for each of the volumes in this series.

And now let's dig in. You have stumbled your way through shifting sand long enough. May these books on Bible doctrine give you just the help you need so that you can stand firmly and finally on a foundation that is solid as rock.

Charles R. Swindoll
Fullerton, California

Part
I

God
the
Father

1 Knowing God: Life's Major Pursuit

Prophets are not easygoing people—never have been, never will be. They are notorious for making us uncomfortable. But they never fail to make us think. Interestingly, most prophets have not been spawned in seminaries, nor have they spent all their lives in churches. Some were first farmers or fishermen. A few of them came from such unlikely places as political arenas and prison wards. One in our generation was both politician and prisoner before he emerged as a prophet.

I'm referring, of course, to Chuck Colson, former White House assistant during Richard Nixon's presidency. You know Colson's story—from the President's confidant to a prison cell, only to emerge as a clear-thinking prophet for our times.

I think the man received some of his best insights while behind bars. And some of the things he writes that stir us into action found their origin during those lonely months he spent in prison. While reading one of his works not long ago, I came across a few paragraphs that speak for themselves. Hold on tight! Like all other prophets, Chuck Colson doesn't mess around.

> For a generation, Western society has been obsessed with the search for self. We have turned the age-old philosophical question about the meaning and purpose of life into a modern growth industry. Like Heinz, there are fifty-seven varieties, and then some: biofeedback, Yoga, creative consciousness, EST, awareness workshops, TA—each fad with an avid following until something new comes along.

Popular literature rides the wave with best-selling titles that guarantee success with everything from making money to firming flabby thighs. This not-so-magnificent obsession to "find ourselves" has spawned a whole set of counterfeit values; we worship fame, success, materialism, and celebrity. We want to "live for success" as we "look out for number one," and we don't mind "winning through intimidation."

However, this "self" conscious world is in desperate straits. Each new promise leads only to a frustrating paradox. The 1970s self-fulfillment fads led to self-absorption and isolation, rather than the fuller, liberated lives they predicted. The technology created to lead humanity to this new promised land may instead obliterate us and our planet in a giant mushroom cloud. Three decades of seemingly limitless affluence have succeeded only in sucking our culture dry, leaving it spiritually empty and economically weakened. Our world is filled with self-absorbed, frightened, hollow people. . . .

And in the midst of all this we have the church—those who follow Christ. For the church, this ought to be an hour of opportunity. The church alone can provide a moral vision to a wandering people; the church alone can step into the vacuum and demonstrate that there is a sovereign, living God who is the source of Truth.

BUT, the church is in almost as much trouble as the culture, for the church has bought into the same value system: fame, success, materialism, and celebrity. We watch the leading churches and the leading Christians for our cues. We want to emulate the best-known preachers with the biggest sanctuaries and the grandest edifices.

Preoccupation with these values has also perverted the church's message. The assistant to one renowned media pastor, when asked the key to his man's success, replied without hesitation, "We give the people what they want." This heresy is at the root of the most dangerous message preached today: the what's-in-it-for-me gospel.

The "victorious Christian life" has become man's victorious life, not God's. A popular daily devotional quotes Psalm 65:9, "The streams of God are filled with water," and paraphrases it, "I fill my mind to overflowing with thoughts of prosperity and success. I affirm that God is my source and

God is unlimited." This is not just a religious adaptation of the look-out-for-number-one, winner-take-all, God-helps-those-who-help-themselves gospel of our culture; it is heresy.[1]

Woven through the fabric of those penetrating words is the revelation of an invisible, insidious disease that has infected and crippled our once-strong nation. It is commonly called "me-ism" . . . a subtle yet consuming passion to please one's self, to exalt "I, me, mine, myself."[2]

Shirley MacLaine, the award-winning actress, granted an interview to the *Washington Post* back in 1977. In that interview she tipped her hand:

> The most pleasurable journey you take is through yourself . . . the only sustaining love is with yourself . . . When you look back on your life and try to figure out where you've been and where you're going, when you look at your work, your love affairs, your marriages, your children, your pain, your happiness—when you examine all that closely, what you really find out is that the only person you really go to bed with is yourself. . . . The only thing you have is working to the consummation of your own identity. And that's what I've been trying to do all my life.[3]

At the risk of sounding terribly narrow and simplistic, I have a message today that represents not just a different approach—but an *opposite* one. I am more convinced than ever that life's major pursuit is not knowing self . . . but knowing God.

As a matter of fact, unless God is the major pursuit of our lives, all other pursuits are dead-end streets, including trying to know ourselves. They won't work. They won't satisfy. They won't result in fulfillment. They won't do for us what we think they're going to do.

You never really begin the process of coming to know yourself until you begin the process of coming to know God. The by-product of such a process is discovering the peace you long for so desperately.

Root Issues

1. Schedule a lunch or dinner with a close Christian friend or your spouse (no kids along, please). The agenda? Thinking out loud about the major goals and *direction* of your life. Are you *really* growing in your knowledge of God as the days and weeks slip by? Are you *honestly* walking more closely with Jesus Christ? If not, why not? What might be keeping you from making this goal number one? What would have to change in your life and schedule to shift your focus and perspective in the coming months? Record these thoughts in your notebook. Be honest, practical, and don't forget to reserve some time in your evening for prayer.

2. Scripture often condemns people because there is "no room for God in their thoughts." Now, let's get down to the nitty-gritty. How often do WE think about our God during the course of a regular, garden-variety work day? How often do you pause (if only for a moment) to consider the reality and nearness and loving concern of your Lord? Talk to several Christians whom you respect about how *they* do it. Be sure to have your notebook handy so that you can save these valuable insights.

3. Spend some extended time in the Word (you'll probably have to schedule it in advance) reading and reflecting on the power and sovereignty of our great God. Select from passages such as: Isaiah 6; 40; Job 38—41; Psalms 8; 19; 24; 31; 46—47; 91; 95; 100; 103—104; 121; 148; Hebrews 1; Revelation 1; 4; 15; 19; 21— 22. You might try reading a number of these passages in a paraphrased version such as *The Living Bible*. As you read, ask the Lord to help you catch a new vision of who He is, what He demands, and what He can accomplish in and through your life as you trust Him.

Extending Your Roots

1. Read again Chuck Colson's quote from his book, *Loving God*. From this paragraph, let's develop your philosophy of life based on knowing God.

(Your philosophy of life explains your existence and is a framework for your personal testimony.)

My Philosophy of Life Based on Knowing God

PAST: Where did I come from?

PRESENT: What is my purpose?

FUTURE: Where am I going?

Taproot

1. Look for opportunities this week to share your philosophy of life and your personal testimony. In the space below, write down the results of this experience.

2 The Wail of a Weeping Prophet

Let's leave a modern-day prophet, step into the time tunnel, and return to an ancient prophet named Jeremiah. He spoke and wrote 2,500 years ago. Perhaps I should say he wept 2,500 years ago. So much so that to this day he's called "the weeping prophet." Dear Jeremiah! If tears had been ink, I think Jeremiah would have had more to write than all the other prophets put together. Here was a man of God who saw way ahead of his time (most prophets do, by the way). He found himself surrounded by a polluted stream of human depravity, lamenting the condition of his people—people who knew better, who had been instructed for centuries to know and walk with their God. But they had deliberately and willfully turned away from the word of their God. Instead of turning to Him, they went after their own pursuits, which resulted in a downward spiral of self-destruction. They had disintegrated into a weak nation, soon to be destroyed by a greater power.

He wrote these tragic words in chapter 9 of the biblical book that bears his name:

> O that my head were waters, and my eyes a foundation of tears, that I might weep day and night for the slain of the daughter of my people! (v. 1).

The scene the prophet paints isn't pretty—but it is realistic. He says, in effect, "My people are goners! They're a pack of wimps. Those who were once known as strong for their God are now weak, emaciated, and about to be destroyed."

If you want to know what Jeremiah really wished to do, read verse 2:

> O that I had in the desert a wayfarers' lodging place; that I might leave my people, and go from them! (v. 2a).

In today's terms, "Oh, that I could escape to a condo in Palm Springs and get out of this mess, this moral filth and carnal pollution in which I'm living." He really wished for the ability to escape.

Why? Disease was everywhere! He names a few of the symptoms. Not the disease yet, just the symptoms:

> For all of them are adulterers, an assembly of treacherous men. "And they bend their tongue like their bow; lies and not truth prevail in the land" [in today's terms the way it would read is "because they are going from bad to worse"] (vv. 2b-3a).

Jeremiah wails, "Everywhere I turn I seek for truth and I hear lies. I look for faithfulness and I find unfaithfulness. I look for people who are gentle, kind, encouraging, and I find treachery, murder, assault, rape. I look in vain to find the things that are to characterize the people of God."

Now the disease—here's the foundational cause:

> "And they do not know Me," declares the Lord (v. 3b).

That may seem like a very simple answer, yet it's profound. A little later the prophet continues to quote his Lord.

> Let not a wise man boast of his wisdom, and let not the mighty man boast of his might, let not a rich man boast of his riches (v. 23).

Now wait. Just pause right there.

You want to know what people pursue when their eyes are on themselves? You've got it right in that statement. They embrace a "counterfeit value system"—the same dead-end pursuit that Chuck Colson described in his book. Human wisdom . . . human might . . . human riches.

I ask you, is this relevant or what? Does that description

sound like today's world? Stop on most any university campus and ask, "What is your goal? What is your plan? Where are you going?" Sometimes the answers will surprise you.

I was on a university campus not long ago. I asked a student, "Where are you going?" He said, "Lunch." I was expecting some great philosophical answer. But aside from a simple answer like that, you will probably hear, "I want to be resourceful" (human wisdom). "I want to be influential" (human might). "I want to be powerful" (human riches). "I want to be successful. I want to wind up top in my company. I want to run things. I want to control people. I want to be in charge. I want to make a name for myself."

We don't read a single comment in verse 23 about the living God. But in the next statement (v. 24) the solution emerges:

> but let him who boasts boast of this, that he understands and knows Me.

Now there's the cure—plain, brief, and simple. What is it that will make an unfaithful man faithful? What is it that will make an influential man who's controlling people a servant? What is it that will cause an individual who has turned to treachery to become gentle and gracious and giving, demonstrating a heart for God? It is understanding and knowing the living God.

Allow me a few moments to take those words apart. The first word, "understands," in verse 24, comes from a verb in the original text that means to have correct "insight" into the nature of the object. In this case, the object is the living God. It also includes the idea of "conducting oneself wisely and dealing prudently." Harris, Archer, and Waltke add, "conforming one's life to the character of God."[1] It's as if he is writing: "To the one who would otherwise turn to his own might and wisdom and riches I offer an alternate plan." It isn't popular. You'll never be in the majority. But you will find the happiness you're pursuing. You'll discover what life is about if you have correct insight into the nature of and conform your life to the character of the living God.

Second, look again at the word "knows." It is a knowledge gained by the senses, not one gained in a rational manner. It's not a knowledge that you can put your hands on, or that you can prove in an experiment or observe with the naked eye. It is a kind of knowledge that involves the inner faculties of the mind, being focused on and motivated by the living God. It's hard to put that in practical terms. It's a faith-kind-of knowledge. When you put the two words together, "understands" and "knows" fully express all the powers and faculties of a human mind being focused on the living God.

Now, how many people do that? I think a better question is: How many people *want* to do that? Start with yourself—do you?

I often look into the faces of successful businessmen and career women, wondering, "Is that person really pursuing a knowledge of God?" I'm occasionally in touch with individuals who are at the top in their companies. And I often meet people who are on their way up that competitive corporate ladder. And I meet students who are making their plans and fitting their education into their ultimate objectives. Frequently, I think: *Does that person really want to know God?*

How about you? do you really want to understand His ways? I'm not referring to the kind of understanding and knowledge that is merely intellectual theology. Not that. I have in mind men and women who see life through the eyes of God, who understand life's circumstances through the lens of God's plan, who accept and believe that whatever is happening has been given by God, permitted by God, and continues under God's personal surveillance . . . that kind of God-understanding and God-awareness.

Now I need to confess something to you. When I sat down to write about God the Father, I thought, *What can I say?* Returning to this theological root is an awesome journey. Much of it is beyond our comprehension.

Reminds me of the time I got a phone call from Goodwill Industries. They wanted me to speak to their group of people. I said to the lady, "What do you think would be a good subject?" She rather flippantly said, "Oh, how about God and the universe and various subjects?" I thought, *Well, that boils it down to basics, doesn't it? God and the universe.*

How can I limit the subject of the living God to a brief chapter in a book? So I decided I wouldn't take the normal approach on this. Most books on doctrine offer page after page on God's attributes. That's helpful and needed, yet most of us have heard such things since we were little kids in Sunday School. So I've decided to approach this subject in a much more practical way. I want to write about the importance of knowing Him. And having done that, I'm going to trust the Spirit of God to motivate you to change your course in life, if that is necessary. And, lest you get the mistaken idea that everything ends with knowing Him, I will address the flip side in the next section—loving Him.

Extending Your Roots

Jeremiah was called by God to be a prophet to Judah. Read Jeremiah, chapter 1 several times and complete the following:

1. A good title for the chapter is:

2. Paraphrase (put in your own words) Jeremiah 1:4-10:

3. List the important people mentioned in chapter 1:

4. Select and memorize a special verse:

5. Define key words and ideas:
Exile (v. 3)_____

Word of the Lord (v. 4)_____
Authority (v. 10)_____
Sacrifices to other gods (v. 16)_____
Overcome (v. 19)_____
Safe (vv. 8,19)_____
Others:_____

6. Application to my life:

7. Knowing God made a difference in Jeremiah's life and ministry.

8. Knowing God makes a difference in my life and ministry by:

— *Taproot* —

1. Continue a study of Jeremiah listing his strengths and weaknesses. Discover why he is called the "weeping prophet."

3 | The Importance of Knowing God

I am convinced that there is nothing more important about us than what we think about God. Here are just a few of the reasons I believe that.

- It shapes our moral and ethical standards.
- It directly affects our response to pain and hardship.
- It motivates our response toward fortune, fame, power, and pleasure.
- It gives us strength when we are tempted.
- It keeps us faithful and courageous when we are outnumbered.
- It enhances our worship and prompts our praise.
- It determines our life-style and dictates our philosophy.
- It gives meaning and significance to relationships.
- It sensitizes our conscience and creates the desire to be obedient.
- It stimulates hope to go on, regardless.
- It enables me to know what to reject and what to respect while I'm riveted to planet Earth.
- It is the foundation upon which EVERYTHING rests!

God has given us a *general revelation* of Himself in the heavens. So much so that more than once in the New Testament Letter to the Romans it states that we're without excuse. He has written His handiwork in the heavens.

> The heavens are telling of the glory of God; and their expanse is declaring the work of His hands (Ps. 19:1).

You look up into the starry skies and you realize, if you make any kind of serious study of those stars, they didn't just tumble into space. The rising of the tide and the lowering of the tide; the dropping of seed into the ground and the growing of plants; the climates, the wind, the weather, the torrential wind currents that sweep across this earth—those things don't "just happen." They are so obviously from the hand of the living God that you have to train yourself *not* to think that way.

In fact, I personally believe you have to teach a child *not* to believe in God. The most natural thing in the world in the heart of a child is to believe that someone outside himself arranged things and keeps them in motion. If you question that, you haven't listened to children lately.

But there's more. There is also *special revelation* in history as well as in Scripture. God specifically reveals Himself in both. All this brings me to capitalize on five reasons it's important to know God.

Knowing God Gives Us the Desire to Be Like Him

Read again Jeremiah's words:

> "But let him who boasts of this, that he understands and knows Me, that I am the Lord who exercises loving kindness, justice, and righteousness on earth; for I delight in these things," declares the Lord (Jer. 9:24).

Interesting, isn't it, that when the Lord talks about Himself, He reveals His attributes, His character traits: lovingkindness, justice, righteousness.

Over in 1 Peter we read that the Lord is holy. In fact, we even read the command, "You shall be holy, for I am holy" (1:16).

The most natural thing in the world is to become like our parents, even when we don't want to become like our parents! Isn't it amazing? I've heard people say, "When I grow up, I'm not gonna be like my father!" Or, "I'm not going to be like my mother." Yet when they grow up, they are just like their father or mother. Why? Because they know their parents; they've been around them. Their mother's or father's thumbprint is indelibly imprinted on their lives.

That's the way it is with God our Father. The more I get to know my God, the more I become like Him. I discover He's holy; I want to be holy. I discover He's good; I want to be better. I discover He's strong; I want to be more confident. I discover He's in control; I don't want to panic my way through life. I don't want to ricochet from one event to another; I want to move through life calmly, consistently. I want to be like my Father. And in order to be like Him, I need to know what He is like.

Knowing God Reveals the
Truth About Ourselves

A glance into the sixth chapter of Isaiah will help support this fact. What a great section of Scripture!

King Uzziah had died. I take it that Isaiah was close to Uzziah the king. He was grieving over his death. And as a result, he went to the place of worship—the same year, perhaps near the same time that Uzziah had died. And while in worship, he observed the living God. Imagine the scene:

> In the year of King Uzziah's death, I saw the Lord sitting on a throne, lofty and exalted, with the train of His robe filling the temple. Seraphim stood above Him, each having six wings; with two he covered his face, and with two he covered his feet, and with two he flew (vv. 1-2).

Here are six-winged creatures, fluttering about the throne of heaven, giving praise to God. And they are saying, "Holy, Holy, Holy, is the Lord of hosts." One is standing saying it, and another answers in antiphonal voice. Still another praises, and another responds. This group praises, and that group responds. The whole throne is filled with His glory.

And having seen the Lord high and lifted up, Isaiah suddenly got a glimpse of *himself*.

> Then I said, "Woe is me, for I am ruined! Because I am a man of unclean lips, and I live among a people of unclean lips" (v. 5).

Perhaps Isaiah struggled with profanity. He was certainly surrounded by a profane-speaking people. And when he saw the holiness of God in all of His splendor, he clapped his hand over his mouth and thought, *How could I be His spokesman with these unclean lips*?

When we study the Lord God we discover He's holy and we're unholy. It doesn't hurt us to know that; it helps us. We discover that He's perfect and we're imperfect . . . He's strong and we're weak . . . He's patient and we're impatient . . . He's impartial, yet we're prejudiced. He's in control, and our lives are often fractured by fear and worry. And something occurs in that contrast that causes His character to overshadow our need. The result is marvelous—the knowledge of the Holy One equips us to see the truth and to change. I cannot explain how it works; I just know it does.

Do you change by spending time with people? Very little. Only a few people can impact you sufficiently to result in your changing for the good. Most people will tell you that you're so far ahead of others that you don't have anything to work on—"nothin' to worry about." Trust me, God won't leave you with that information! He'll help you see yourself—your strengths and certainly your weaknesses. And every time you turn to His Word, you'll see another flaw, another need, another weakness that needs to be addressed. God always tells us the truth. And it is the truth that sets us free! When we see ourselves as we really are, we are prompted to lean on Him and to trust Him to make us like He is.

Knowing God Enables Us to Interpret Our World

Toward the end of the fourth chapter of Daniel, we bump into a rather remarkable individual. The man's name is Nebuchadnezzar. He is the king of Babylon. In great arrogance the king lived as though he needed no one else. Full of conceit, he is strutting around the kingdom with his thumbs under his suspenders saying, "How great I am. How wonderful I am. Look at this kingdom I've built. What a magnificent person I have become. Everybody, together, say it with me again and again, 'Nebuchadnezzar,' Let's all say together." Then, very suddenly, he lost his mind.

> Immediately the word concerning Nebuchadnezzar was fulfilled; and he was driven away from mankind and began eating grass like cattle, and his body was drenched with the dew of heaven, until his hair had grown like eagles' feathers and his nails like birds' claws (v. 33).

It means just what it says. This once-great man is reduced to a wild beast, living out in the field through day and night, with claws like an eagle and long hair. What a terrible, insane existence!

I can't fully explain my next statement. I can only tell you it's often true: For some people, it takes insanity to come to the end of themselves and to find God. That's the way it was with Nebuchadnezzar. Not all breakdowns are the end of a person's life. Sometimes they are the beginning, which means we should perhaps call them break-*ups*. One day the Nebuchadnezzar-beast paused in the midst of its grazing and looked up toward heaven. A shaft of light broke through into the darkened mind. As the king described it:

> But at the end of the period I, Nebuchadnezzar, raised my eyes toward heaven and my reason returned to me, and I blessed the Most High and praised and honored Him who lives forever; [he used to praise and honor himself];
> For His dominion is an everlasting dominion,
> And His kingdom endures from generation to generation.
> And all the inhabitants of the earth are accounted as nothing,
> But He does according to His will in the host of heaven
> And among the inhabitants of earth;
> And no one can ward off His hand
> Or say to Him, "What hast Thou done?"
> At that time my reason returned to me (vv. 34-36).

It's the thirty-fifth verse that interests me.

> And all the inhabitants of the earth are accounted as nothing,
> But He does according to His will in the host of heaven

> And among the inhabitants of earth;
> And no one can ward off His hand
> Or say to Him, "What hast Thou done?"

Once Nebuchadnezzar saw God in all His sovereignty and glory, his whole perspective changed. He saw the earth as under God's control. His pride vanished as he realized that God was the One calling the shots, not himself.

I remember that during my pastoral internship many years ago I happened to come across Daniel 4. That summer I was studying the Book of Daniel. And I'll never forget struggling over the sovereignty of God. I battled with it. I wrestled with God about it. I'd been taught to reject it, to resist it, to turn it off as heresy . . . yet, here in Daniel 4 I had to face it.

And you know what? I could resist it no longer. In fact, I finally embraced it.

I began to experience a peace like you can't believe. A calm swept over me. I distinctly remember saying to Pastor Ray Stedman of the church where I was an intern, "I gotta tell ya, Ray, that doctrine has changed my life this summer." Ray, who had long since come to realize that same truth, grinned from ear to ear and said, "Chuck, that is wonderful! It will be a comfort to you throughout your ministry." He was right.

When you get hold of the knowledge of God and begin to see that He is in charge, you won't panic every time you read the paper. You won't give up hope because there's an earthquake somewhere. You won't live in the fear of terrorism or possible disease.

In fact, you'll be able to sort of sing your way through the business section, editorial page—even the sports page! Why? Because you know the God who is in control of all things.

People have this weird idea that God is tentatively sitting on the edge of heaven going, "Ooh! Oh, no! How am I gonna handle this? HELP!" My friend, that's *not* the God of the Scriptures. That isn't the living God who holds everything in His hands. He may be invisible, but He's in touch. You may not be able to see Him, but He is in control. And that includes *you*—your circumstances. That includes what you've just lost. That includes what you've just gained. That includes all of life . . . past, present, future.

Knowing God Makes Us Stronger and More Secure

Goodness knows, we need this! Daniel 11:32 says:

> And by smooth words he will turn to godlessness those who act wickedly toward the covenant, but the people who know their God will display strength and take action.

This verse emerges from a tough setting. It's a scene of conflict and warfare. There's a battle going on between good and evil. And right in the middle of the verse, Daniel inserts:

> but the people who know their God will display strength and take action.

James Boice writes these words about the strength of our God.

> We do not have a strong church today nor do we have *many* strong Christians. We can trace the cause to an acute lack of sound spiritual knowledge. Why is the church weak? Why are individual Christians weak? It's because they have allowed their minds to become conformed to the "spirit of this age," with its mechanistic, godless thinking. They have forgotten what God is like and what He promises to do for those who trust Him. Ask an average Christian to talk about God. After getting past the expected answers you will find that his god is a little god of vacillating sentiments. He is a god who would like to save the world but who cannot. He would like to restrain evil, but somehow he finds it beyond his power. So he has withdrawn into semiretirement, being willing to give good advice in a grandfatherly sort of way, but for the most part he has left his children to fend for themselves in a dangerous environment.
>
> Such a god is not the God of the Bible . . . the God of the Bible is not weak; He is strong. He is all-mighty. Nothing

happens without His permission or apart from His purposes—even evil. Nothing disturbs or puzzles Him. His purposes are always accomplished. Therefore those who know Him rightly act with boldness, assured that God is with them to accomplish His own desirable purposes in their lives.[1]

I want to ask you a direct question. Isn't it true, more often than not, that the God you picture in your mind is old, has a long beard—and maybe leans on a cane? Isn't that true? You picture Him standing in the north with His cheeks pushing out as He blows real hard, right? Sure you do. He wears a robe, has big toes, sandals. He's not too sure about modern things like advanced nuclear physics, dense packs, laser beams, and electronic computers. He's more of a kind old grandfather that is gonna be there when you need Him, and you can trust Him because He is wise and generous. He could handle things yesterday and maybe He could handle most things today. But He's sort of losing touch.

If that's your God, then listen to me: THAT IS HERESY!

It is nothing short of HERESY to think of God like that. He isn't old; He is eternal. He isn't intimidated; He is omnipotent. Computers don't bother Him; He is omniscient! The nuclear warheads don't have Him worried! He is sovereign.

So things aren't out of hand! He's in control. He can handle it. And what's more, He can handle you. He knows you thoroughly. He even knows the number of the hairs on your head (and for some of you, that's no big deal). He's got everything wired! He's got it all together! He is the sovereign God of the universe and He's never once lost control. He strengthens and He secures His people. Those who know their God operate in such a context of confidence, they can face whatever . . . and "display strength and take action."

See the value of knowing God? See what it does to your perspective? See how much calmer you become? Lift your eyes. Behold His glory high and lifted up. Worthy is the Lamb that was slain to give power and authority over this place. His kingdom will not fail. That's our God.

Now, I've saved the best till last. Why is it important to know Him?

Knowing God Introduces Us to the Eternal Dimension of Existence

Look at John 17:3. Jesus is praying to the Father as He says:

> And this is eternal life, that they may know Thee, the only true God, and Jesus Christ whom Thou has sent.

Knowing God introduces me to the invisible world of God's kingdom. I see through eyes that aren't given to everyone. We read elsewhere:

> Things which eye has not seen and ear has not heard, and which have not entered the heart of man, all that God has prepared for those who love Him (1 Cor. 2:9).

The natural person isn't born with this kind of insight. It's given at the new birth. That's why I often talk about coming to know Jesus Christ, believing in the Lord Jesus Christ, turning one's life over to Christ, coming to one's heart's door, opening it by faith, and saying, "Jesus Christ, come into my life. Take charge." Because when He comes in, He introduces us to an eternal dimension for living. And that perspective lifts the mind ABOVE the present, irksome details of life. What we gain is an eternal dimension of life.

Extending Your Roots

A character study involves the characteristics of a person, rather than the person himself.

King Nebuchadnezzar of Babylon was a ruler who decided it was profitable to cooperate with his conquests in some things. He mainly allowed them to worship their gods.

Using the Book of Daniel as a basic resource, find out what the Bible says about this king's particular characteristics.

Other references for study are 2 Kings 24—25; 2 Chronicles 36; Jeremiah 21—52.

1. What changes came into Nebuchadnezzar's life when he came to know God?

2. What lessons from his life can you apply to your life?

What does it mean for you to know God?

 *Taproot*

Reread the five reasons knowing God is important. Write a personal response to each reason.

1. Knowing God gives us the desire to be like Him. I will:

2. Knowing God reveals the truth about ourselves. I will:

3. Knowing God enables us to interpret our world. I will:

4. Knowing God makes us stronger and more secure. I will:

5. Knowing God introduces us to the eternal dimension of existence. I will:

4 | Finally, Some Essential Facts

As we have considered five reasons to know God, I must confess to a little fear. My fear doesn't relate to what I've communicated—but to what you might do with it. You might have the idea that if you take pen in hand and open the Bible and start in Genesis and work your way through to Revelation, you'll have it all put together. You'll not only understand everything about God, you'll understand all the mysteries, right? Wrong!

> Oh, the depth of the riches both of the wisdom and knowledge of God! How unsearchable are His judgments and unfathomable His ways! (Rom. 11:33).

Remember those words when you travel down the road in hopes of understanding and knowing your God. Realize in advance that you will come to some streets that are mysterious and unfathomable. Don't let the mystery surprise you or disturb you. God planned it that way.

Some Incomprehensible Subjects

It occurs to me that there are several theological thoughts that are incomprehensible. Four come to mind.

Trinity

There is one God yet three distinct persons. The Godhead is coequal, coeternal, coexistent: God the Father, God the Son, God the Holy Spirit. Much of that remains a profound mystery. Don't lose sleep if you cannot unravel the truth of the Trinity.

Finally, Some Essential Facts

Glory

The Trinity has to do with the *person* of God. Glory has to do with the *presence* of God. It has something to do with light—with blinding brilliance. The people sensed His presence in the tabernacle and the temple because the light of His glory was there. That same glory of God was later lifted from the place of worship and removed because of the unbelief of the people. There is something terribly mysterious about the glory of God, revealed through Scripture. Don't weary yourself trying to unscrew the inscrutable.

Sovereignty

This has to do with the *plan* of God. Certainly, He is in control of all things; yet, even though He is perfectly holy, sin is present. He permits it. He allows it. Without being contaminated by the sin, our Holy God is working out His plan. If you want to engage in a futile study, try to reconcile those things. No, seriously, quit trying to reconcile it! Take it by faith!

Majesty

This relates to the Father's *position*. He is unseen and will remain unseen throughout eternity. I'm not sure if we will ever see God the Father, even in a glorified state, and yet He's there in all of His glory. His majestic position will never be diminished—and yet I'm sure we'll never be able to grasp it on this earth. Just believe it. And bow before His almighty majesty.

Even though we may not ever understand *everything* about God, there are some things about Him that we *can* understand. These things are very practical and absolutely essential. Let me close this part of our study with them. None of these things are mysterious. They can be grasped and applied.

• *God is pleased when we walk by faith.* The Bible is full of that fact. Nothing pleases the Lord more than when we walk by faith.

• *God is glorified when we worship in truth.* When I come

across something that I can't handle or explain, He's pleased when I trust Him to get me through it. And when I gather in an assembly with other believers—or all alone— and I worship my God, He's glorified in it.

• *God is our Father when we believe in His Son—and not until.* Scripture never teaches that God is the Father of everyone, even though He graciously gives rain and sun to all on this earth. By grace, He becomes the Father of those who believe in His Son.

If you read this book, go out and buy a big study Bible, and start to work on discovering just the *facts* about God, you've really grasped only part of what I've tried to communicate.

True knowledge affects the way we live, affects our attitude, affects our heart, our response, and it changes our direction. It alters the way we make decisions. It even takes away our worries. It brings us face to face with the truth of God and what He says about Himself. Perhaps that best explains why God's prophets have always been so intense and so unbending—and why their message has never failed to cut through the veneer of all the things that keep us from knowing the living God.

Knowing God is life's major pursuit, but that's only half the story. Loving God is our ultimate response. And that's what the next section is all about.

Extending Your Roots

1. Review the three facts that we *can* understand about knowing God.

(1) God is pleased when we walk by faith.
(2) God is glorified when we worship in truth.
(3) God is our Father when we believe in His Son . . . and not until then.

2. Using a concordance, verify in Scripture each one of these facts. Select several references and reflect on who God

is, what He demands, and what He can accomplish through your life.

3. A word study is a search for understanding Bible words. The purpose of the study is to learn as much as possible about what the biblical writers meant by the words they used.

Good resources for a word study are a concordance, a Bible dictionary, and other Bible translations.

Examine these four words:

- *Trinity*
- *Glory*
- *Sovereignty*
- *Majesty*

Answer these questions about each word:

(1) What does the word mean?

(2) How many times does the word occur in the Bible?

(3) Which writers used the word?

 *Taproot*

1. Interview older Christians on the subject of knowing God.

Ask the following questions during the interview:

- When did you begin knowing God?
- Would you consider knowing Him as the major pursuit of your life?

● Can you stop knowing Him?

Conclude the interview by talking about God and what He has done for you in your pursuit to know Him.

5 Loving God: Our Ultimate Response

There are not enough people who encourage us in life. As a matter of fact, I find that a majority of people have a way of discouraging us rather than affirming us and offering us fresh confidence to go on.

John Powell tells a true story that vividly illustrates this fact. It happened to one of his friends who was vacationing in the Bahamas.

He saw a large and restless crowd gathered on a pier. Upon investigation he discovered that the object of all the attention was a young man making the last-minute preparations for a solo journey around the world in a homemade boat. Without exception everyone on the pier was vocally pessimistic. All were actively volunteering to tell the ambitious sailor all the things that could possibly go wrong. "The sun will broil you! . . . You won't have enough food! . . . That boat of yours won't withstand the waves in a storm! . . . You'll never make it!"

When my friend heard all these discouraging warnings to the adventurous young man, he felt an irresistible desire to offer some optimism and encouragement. As the little craft began drifting away from the pier towards the horizon, my friend went to the end of the pier, waving both arms wildly like semaphores spelling confidence. He kept shouting: "Bon voyage! You're really something! We're with you! We're proud of you! Good luck, brother!"[1]

Can't you picture that scene? Everybody on the pier saying, "You'll never make it, man . . . that boat of yours is sure to sink!" And here stands one fellow waving his arms, shouting, "Go for ĭt! You can do it! We believe in you!"

What's true about life in general is also true about the Christian life in particular. You and I are in the little boat. And that little boat has put out to sea. We are on our journey toward knowing and obeying God. Have you noticed how few there are who stand alongside as we push out into the sea, saying, "Good for you! Go for it! You can make it! You're on the right track! God be with you!"

I feel like we need many more who say such affirming things to all who desire to grow in their knowledge of God and the doctrines of His Word. In fact, as I write this book I think of myself on the pier cheering you on because I believe in your journey. And I believe that if you have made the decision to know God fully and to walk with Him obediently and to learn His truths thoroughly, He will honor that decision. He, too, applauds your determination to return to your theological roots and discover the ocean of truth that stretches out before you. Never lose that love for knowledge! Never stop exploring in this adventure of faith! My hope is that each of these chapters will encourage you as well as inform you.

We have spent several chapters thinking about the importance of knowing God, which I've called life's major pursuit. Let's consider the other side of the same coin—loving God, which is clearly our ultimate response.

Tucked away in the fifth book of the Bible is a profound statement and a wonderful command. I want you to see both statement and command together in Deuteronomy 6, verses 4 and 5. The command is preceded by the statement. Let's look first at the statement, which talks about *knowing* God, and then let's observe the command, which addresses the importance of *loving* God.

Deuteronomy 6:4 is one of the most familiar statements in all of Jewish liturgy:

> Hear, O Israel! The Lord is our God, the Lord is one!

You can't see it in the English, but in the Hebrew that

word *one* conveys the idea of "one in multiple," one as in a "cluster" or "group." *Echad* is the Hebrew word for one, as in a cluster of grapes. "The Lord our God is one—one in Father, one in Son, one in Spirit." Moses says, "Hear, O Israel, and come to know Him as your only God." That statement had to do with knowing God. Now, the command:

> And you shall love the Lord your God with all your heart and with all your soul and with all your might (v. 5).

How significant was this? He now explains its importance:

> And these words, which I am commanding you today, shall be on your heart; and you shall teach them diligently to your sons and shall talk of them when you sit in your house and when you walk by the way and when you lie down and when you rise up. And you shall bind them as a sign on your hand and they shall be as frontals on your forehead. And you shall write them on the doorposts of your house and on your gates (vv. 6-9).

God is saying, "This is something I want you to put on your heart, men and women. And then as I bring children into your family, these are the things I want you to teach them. Not simply as an intellectual exercise, but I want it to be in the warp and woof of your lives. I want it to take place when you lie down at night and when you get up. When you walk, when you play, when you work. I want these things to characterize your life-style. I want you to model knowing Me and loving Me with all your heart, with all your soul, with all your might. And I want your children to absorb the same convictions, so that they will have that impression even when you're gone."

Every once in a while my wife and I talk about how life will be in our family when both of us are gone. I'm sure you who are parents have discussed the same. Cynthia and I are in agreement. We are in great hopes that our children will have learned by our model that there was nothing on earth more important to their mother and dad than knowing God and loving Him with all their heart and soul and might. If they will have gotten that impression, we will have accomplished a major part of our job. You see, children don't automatically realize the value of knowing God and loving Him. They need it modeled. They need those things woven into the fabric of their childhood memories.

How important was it for the Israelites? A brief history lesson will be worth the effort. Those people were right on the verge of the land of Canaan—the land that "flowed with milk and honey," the promised land. But what you may not remember is that it was crawling with idolaters. An idolatrous atmosphere covered the territory where they would soon be living. Shortly, Moses would die, leaving only the memory of his instruction in their minds. Once they invaded and conquered Canaan, they would begin to rear their families in homes they didn't build, eating from vineyards they didn't plant, drinking from cisterns they didn't dig. From a nomadlike existence they would gain instant affluence.

So Moses is concerned that those simple people who had cultivated a simple walk of faith might be blown away by the impact of idolatry and affluence, which could diminish their love for God. That explains why he told them to print His words on the doorposts of their houses, to write them on their hands and foreheads. He didn't want them ever to forget that they were people who knew and loved Jehovah God.

> And He brought us out from there in order to bring us in, to give us the land which He had sworn to our fathers. So the Lord commanded us to observe all these statutes, to fear the Lord our God for our good always and for our survival, as it is today (vv. 23-24).

Let me make a suggestion: Underscore those last two prepositional phrases in red, "for our good" . . . "for our survival."

I don't know how many people I've met who lived under the false impression that when God makes a command He's trying to take away our fun. On the contrary, when God gives us a command, it's always for our good—and it's often for our survival. If you want to do what is good and what will help you survive, then get to know your God and love Him with all your heart, soul, and mind.

You'll remember in the previous section that I didn't give you six steps on how to know God. That was on purpose. Knowing God doesn't occur like that. It isn't a mechanical, step-by-step process. It's a lifetime pursuit. What it really requires is a day-by-day commitment in one's head and one's heart. A commitment that says, "Today I'm going to know God better. Today I'm going to love God more. This is going to become a regular, major pursuit of my life."

And piece by piece, little by little, day after day, it will begin to permeate your whole frame of reference. That's what Moses wanted for the Israelites, and that's what God wants for us.

 *Root Issues*

1. Who are you *encouraging* in the Christian life? Are there one or more individuals who feel the courage to dig deeper, hang on tighter, or look heavenward because of your regular counsel and concern? How about someone *outside* your family circle? Who, for instance, could you encourage with a note or letter? Make it a goal to write such a note this week. It doesn't need to be elaborate . . . just an appropriate Scripture, or a thought about the love and faithfulness of the Lord—and your genuine expression of support. "I care" goes a long, long way.

2. If you have children, project yourself ahead to that day when they will be on their own—even when you may be off the scene. What will they have learned about the priority of loving God by *observing* the lives of their mom or dad? If you find yourself troubled by your "glimpse into the future," discuss your concerns with your spouse or a close Christian friend. How can you better *model* the priority of loving God?

3. Read Psalm 40, especially the first three verses. Can

you remember the last "pit" you found yourself in—knee-deep in the muck—your heart almost breaking (v. 2)? Do you recall how the Lord heard your cry and reached down to deliver you? Why not follow David's example and *write* about it? There is something uniquely powerful about *writing* one's praise and gratitude to God—even if you and God are the only ones who ever see it! Open your notebook to a fresh page and take time to actually write a special letter to God, just pouring out all your joy and appreciation for what He has done. And even if you *still* find yourself in a pit, write to your Father about it. Open your heart to Him. Tell Him how you're trusting Him to deliver you. This is one letter that will be received and read!

Extending Your Roots

"There are not enough people who encourage us in life." Thus begins chapter 6. A response to that statement might be, "We don't know how."

1. Two role -models are given in the Book of Acts to demonstrate the encourager and the encouragee. John Mark needed an encourager; Barnabas knew what to do. Study the Scripture passages and discover how encouragement works.

Mark
the discouraged
Read Acts 12:25—13:13 and
    15:36-37.
He is also mentioned
    in four other books.

Barnabas
the encouraged
Acts 9:27—15:39
He is also mentioned
    in three other books.

2. Locate these references using a concordance. Take a look at yourself. Are you a Mark or a Barnabas?

3. Read 1 Thessalonians 5:11.

Loving God: Our Ultimate Response

 *Taproot*

1. The apostle Paul gave several examples of how we can encourage others. Read 1 Thessalonians 5:11-23. List at least five suggestions.

2. Write a note or make a visit this week to someone who needs encouragement. Record what happened.

6 God of Grace, God of Mercy

Let's turn our attention from Deuteronomy to the Psalms, from history to poetry, four hundred years later, during the reign of King David. Deuteronomy looked ahead, the Psalms look back. Moses anticipated the things on the horizon, and David responded by recording a number of the events that transpired.

I told you at the beginning of this book that this would not be your basic book on Bible doctrine. Here is a case in point. Take time to let your heart be encouraged in God. In the next few pages I want us to graze through several psalms. We'll see God at work as He came to the people's rescue for their good and for their survival. And then later on, we'll focus on the poet himself—David. We'll see how God brought him through difficult personal situations. And we'll see how David's heart welled over in response to this great love of God.

My hope is that these few pages we spend in the Psalms will stir up your faith and whet your appetite to trust God as you have never trusted Him before. After all, no one is more trustworthy than He! What will stand out in the Psalms is that the people, in every case, had no other one to lean on but God. They had no arsenal of weapons. They had no defense, not even a flag to fly. All they had was the living, trustworthy, faithful God! And the psalmist talks about how He came through time after time after time. The absence of all other substitutes forced them to lean hard on their God. When they did, He showed Himself strong in grace and glory.

God of Grace, God of Mercy

Psalm 31. This is a good place to start. Look at the protection God provided:

> In Thee, O Lord, I have taken refuge; Let me never be ashamed; In Thy righteousness deliver me. Incline Thine ear to me, rescue me quickly; Be Thou to me a rock of strength, A stronghold to save me. For Thou art my rock and my fortress; For Thy name's sake Thou wilt lead me and guide me. Thou wilt pull me out of the net which they have secretly laid for me; For Thou art my strength (vv. 1-4).

Notice there is no other strength, no other source of encouragement, no other protection—only the Lord. Hence, David says, "It's You, Lord, I turn to."

A little later on he writes this prayer:

> Be gracious to me, O Lord, for I am in distress; My eye is wasted away from grief, my soul, and my body also. For my life is spent with sorrow, And my years with sighing; My strength has failed because of my iniquity, And my body has wasted away. Because of all my adversaries, I have become a reproach (vv. 9-11*a*).

Ever had this experience? Just read on and you'll feel it with him.

> I have become a reproach, Especially to my neighbors, And an object of dread to my acquaintances; Those who see me in the street flee from me. I am forgotten as a dead man, out of mind, I am like a broken vessel. For I have heard the slander of many, Terror is on every side; While they took counsel together against me, They schemed to take away my life (vv. 11*b*-13).

Look at the man. "Lord, I am at Your mercy. I have no defense. I am outnumbered. I am surrounded. And in myself, I am intimidated." But the point here is this, "But, Lord, O God, I know You. I trust You to get me through this." Read on.

> But as for me, I trust in Thee, O Lord, I say, "Thou art my God." My times are in Thy hand; Deliver me from the hand of my enemies, and from those who persecute me (vv. 14-15).

Haven't you experienced holding on to things, gripping things, keeping them near, playing your cards close to your vest, protecting them, not wanting God to take them? They were important things to you, things you'd leaned on for strength, almost as if they were idols, right? And slowly, agonizingly, the Lord pried your fingers loose and you had to let go. I love how Corrie ten Boom used to put it. She used to say, "Vell, I've learned to hold every ting loosely, because it hurts ven God pries my fingers apart and takes dem from me."

An anonymous poet said it this way:

One by one God took them from me,
All the things I valued most,
Till I was empty-handed,
Every glittering toy was lost.

And I walked earth's highways grieving
In my rags and poverty
Til I heard His voice inviting
"Lift those empty hands to Me."

So I turned my hands toward heaven,
And He filled them with a store
Of His own transcendent riches
Till they could contain no more.

And at last I comprehended,
With my stupid mind and dull
That God could not pour His riches
Into hands already full.

Let it go. Trust Him. Love Him. Remind yourself that He's trustworthy. He won't hang you out to dry. Let others slander. Let them say those things against you. He knows you have integrity. Release your defense. Quit trying to fight back—give the battle to the Lord! That's the message of Psalm 31. Trust in no substitutes, seek no other refuge, lean on no other crutch but the living God. Love Him as you love no one else on earth. I dare you!

Psalm 37. Here is another grand statement of faith in this gracious, glorious God. Consider the inner strength, the peace that He alone gives. Let's work our way through the first nine verses.

> Do not fret because of evildoers, Be not envious toward wrongdoers. For they will wither quickly like the grass, And fade like the green herb (vv. 1-2).

Ever find yourself envious of the evildoers? Isn't it amazing how those who do wrong get away with murder, and you and I who do right can't even get away with taking a quarter out of the phone booth? Isn't it remarkable? Somehow God zaps us with such guilt we have to return and stick the quarterback in the slot so we can live with ourselves.

> Trust in the Lord, and do good; Dwell in the land and cultivate faithfulness. Delight yourself in the Lord; and He will give you the desires of your heart. Commit your way to the Lord, Trust also in Him, and He will do it. And He will bring forth your righteousness as the light, And your judgment as the noonday (vv. 3-6).

You see, our God knows us so well. When we begin to fret because of one who prospers in wickedness, then anger replaces peace. That anger boils over into wrath, and wrath begins to consume us. So He says again, "Do not fret yourself. It leads only to evildoing" (v. 8). How much better to focus on letting God do our defending.

> For evildoers will be cut off, But those who wait for the Lord, they will inherit the land (v. 9).

Observe an illustration David uses:

> I have seen a violent, wicked man Spreading himself like a luxuriant tree in its native soil (v. 35).

Can't you picture it? "I've seen this big hulk of a man, evil in his ways, with blood dripping from his fingers, planning wickedness, doing wrong, growing larger, more powerful, more intimidating."

Then he passed away, and lo, he was no more; I sought for him, but he could not be found. Mark the blameless man, and behold the upright; For the man of peace will have a posterity. But transgressors will be altogether destroyed; The posterity of the wicked will be cut off. But the salvation of the righteous is from the Lord; He is their strength in time of trouble. And the Lord helps them, and delivers them; He delivers them from the wicked, and saves them, Because they take refuge in Him (vv. 36-40).

What magnificent words of hope! I have a feeling they increase your pulse as you read them. Here's why. You don't walk close to God very long before you become the face on someone's dart board, the object of someone's resentment and wrath, even though you really did no wrong to that person. For all the right reasons and the purest of motives, you did what you did and you have been misunderstood. It's a very tender place to be.

Here's the major point of this psalm: Your knowledge of God and your love for God will be on display in how you respond to the other person's treatment. Rather than diminishing His glory, let your light shine! God will honor such a response.

Psalm 46. We cannot—we dare not—ignore this, another statement of faith.

God is our refuge and strength, a very present help in trouble (v. 1).

My favorite word in that opening line is "present." "A very present help." Right now.

Therefore we will not fear, though the earth should change, And though the mountains slip into the heart of the sea; Though its waters roar and foam, Though the mountains quake at its swelling pride. Selah (vv. 2-3).

Someone has suggested that each time the word "Selah" appears in the Psalms it's time to think, "pause and let that sink in—drink that in." Drink what in? This: "God is our refuge and strength, a very present help in trouble."

My sister Luci was, for some time after she graduated, a

field representative for her alma mater. And while she was traveling around the Southwest making contact with potential students, she, of course, had a number of interesting experiences as a single woman.

On one unforgettable occasion she noticed that she was being followed by a vehicle. Since it was getting dark and she was alone, she became increasingly uneasy. She decided she would turn in for the night, and so she drove into this rather small town and began searching for a motel. She noticed that the car behind her did the same. As she made several unusual turns, the car following her did, too. So she knew for sure she was being followed. She quickly pulled into a motel, got out, and registered. She noticed the lights of the other car down the road about a half a block away. Her heart was beating in her throat. After quickly signing the register, she got the key and jumped into her car, drove around to the room, grabbed her bags, and ran inside. She quickly locked every possible lock there was on the door and then breathed a sigh of relief.

While preparing herself for bed, she needed to take a shower. While she was stepping out of the shower, she noticed that the venetian blind was up a little on one end, and she suddenly had this horrible sense of fear that she was being watched, that this person who followed her was right outside the window. And Luci later said to me, "I didn't know what to do. I was defenseless, I was all alone. If he were outside and if he had broken in, I couldn't have protected myself. Then for some strange reason I looked down and noticed that someone had slipped a piece of paper under the glass on top of the chest of drawers."

These words were written on that paper:

> Come to Me, all who are weary and heavy laden, and I will give you rest. Take My yoke upon you, and learn from Me, for I am gentle and humble in heart; and you shall find rest for your souls (Matt. 11:28-29).

She said when she saw those verses, she was enveloped with an enormous sense of relief that surged over her. With the towel wrapped around her, she marched over and yanked that venetian blind down, put on her pajamas, turned the lights off, got into bed, and immediately fell asleep . . . zzzzzzzz! And not another thing happened that night.

There is something *remarkable* about the Word of God when it's taken literally and applied to your situation. It works, friends! It works! It isn't voodoo. It isn't magic. It isn't some kind of divine aura you place on someone else. It is the living and abiding Word of God. It is His *present* help. It is the testimony of His strength in your life. It's as if He is pleading, "Take it. Believe it. Apply it. Love Me for it." And it works! Stories like that could be multiplied all over the family of God.

When we make the Lord alone our single source of protection or solitary refuge, He shows Himself strong, doesn't He? And then who gets the glory? When He comes through, all you can do is say, "Praise be to the Lord . . . He did it again!"

Now, the best part of the whole process is this: As He proves Himself strong when we need Him, the most natural response on our part is love, "Oh, how I love this One who sees me through. He is truly worthy of my worship. My Maker, Defender, Redeemer, and Friend!"

Extending Your Roots

1. Reading the suggested psalms and locate the words or phrases that cause us to trust our loving God.

Psalm	*Words or phrases*	*What God does for us*
3		
5		
20		
27		

2. List some recent ways you have trusted God to help you.

God of Grace, God of Mercy

1. Write your own psalm to your loving God.

7 Man of Gratitude, Man of Love

Now I want to show you how this grateful man responded to his Lord's gracious dealings. I'm referring, of course, to David.

Psalm 18. He has been delivered from the hands of his enemies. He has been rescued from Saul's pursuit again and again. He is now safe in some forlorn place. I don't know if he's in the open wilderness or in a narrow cave, but the best part of all is this: He is safe. And once safe, he *has* to write a song, he *has* to testify of his gratitude in song. All who write music can understand such an impulse of praise. He begins:

I love Thee, O Lord, my strength (v. 1).

Here is why he loved his Lord so passionately:

The Lord is my rock and my fortress and my deliverer, My God, my rock, in whom I take refuge; My shield and the horn of my salvation, my stronghold. I call upon the Lord, who is worthy to be praised, And I am saved from my enemies. The cords of death encompassed me, And the torrents of ungodliness terrified me. The cords of Sheol surrounded me; The snares of death confronted me. In my distress I called upon the Lord, And cried to my God for help; He heard my voice out of His temple, And my cry for help before Him came into His ears (vv. 2-6).

The response of love concludes the same psalm:

The Lord lives, and blessed be my rock; And exalted be the God of my salvation, The God who executes vengeance for me, And subdues peoples under me. He delivers me from my enemies; Surely Thou dost lift me above those who rise up against me; Thou dost rescue me from the violent man. Therefore I will give thanks (vv. 46-49).

He said at the beginning, "I love You, O Lord." He says toward the ending, "I thank You, Lord."

Now the scene isn't always that simple and objective. Sometimes we will do wrong. Sometimes our situation is deserved. Sometimes we will fail. We will stumble. David stumbled terribly.

When I mention the name David, unfortunately many people think first of his failure—and it is a glaring one. At the height of his career, he stumbled into lust. The lust turned into open adultery, the adultery led to murder, the murder led to deception—in fact, almost a year of lying to his people. Don't you know the word spread in his kingdom? Can't you imagine how they whispered about him in the alleys and in the homes around the palace? It was obvious he had married Bathsheba. And it was obvious as they counted back over the months that she had had the baby in less than nine months, in those days a slanderous thing. All of that was clear to the people. During those awful months, he slumped into an enormous depression.

When he came out on the other side, after he repented, he wrote another song.

Psalm 32. He has compromised his walk with the Lord, he has given into lust, murder, deception. We can hardly imagine his misery. Verse 3:

> When I kept silent about my sin, my body wasted away
> Through my groaning all day long.

Ever had that happen? Ever been so stubborn in your iniquity that you refused to confess it, resulting in your beginning to suffer physically for it? How many illnesses really can be traced to sin!

> For day and night Thy hand was heavy upon me; My vitality was drained away as with the fever heat of summer. Selah. I acknowledged my sin to Thee, And my iniquity I did not hide; I said, "I will confess my transgression to the Lord"; and Thou didst forgive the guilt of my sin. Selah. (vv. 4-5).

Now look back at verses 1 and 2. You'll read the response of a forgiven man.

> How blessed is he whose transgression is forgiven, Whose sin is covered! How blessed is the man to whom the Lord does not impute iniquity, And in whose spirit there is no deceit!

"How blessed I am, how forgiven, how clean!"

You know what's happened? He's claimed God's cleansing. He's experienced God's forgiveness. And as a result, his love is expressed in gratitude. "I see my wrong. I accept it as wrong, and I lay it before You." Don't dare overlook the fact that God took away the guilt as well as the sin.

Psalm 40.

> I waited patiently for the Lord; And He inclined to me, and heard my cry. He brought me up out of the pit of destruction, out of the miry clay (vv. 1-2a).

This "pit of destruction" can mean many things to us today. It may mean a depression. It may represent a period of time where you wandered. It may be a period of unexplainable sorrow in your life, a series of losses and grief. It may be the loss of health, a terminal illness. You put your pit in this situation. David left it undefined.

> He brought me up out of the pit of destruction, out of the miry clay; And He set my feet upon a rock making my footsteps firm. And He put a new song in my mouth, a song of praise to our God; Many will see and fear, And will trust in the Lord.

> How blessed is the man who has made the Lord his trust (vv. 2-4).

I'm thinking of that grand hymn:

> Guide me, O Thou great Jehovah,
> Pilgrim through this barren land;
> I am weak, but Thou are mighty;
> Hold me with Thy pow'rful hand;
> Bread of heaven, Bread of heaven,
> Feed me till I want no more,
> Feed me till I want no more.[1]

The last part of the third stanza says, "Song of praises, songs of praises I will ever give to Thee." The heart that loves God is a heart that bursts forth in songs of praise. It is marvelously spontaneous. It is wonderful to have your heart so in love with your Lord that the only way to express it is to sing it. "Songs of praises I will ever give to Thee." What a response of love!

 Extending Your Roots

David, the shepherd boy/king, was a grateful man who loved God. Many significant happenings in his life are expressed in the Psalms.

1. Read the Scripture reference and the psalm and then record the happening in his life and what David learned about God from his experience.

Scripture Reference	Psalm	Happening	What He Learned
1 Samuel 21	34; 56		
1 Samuel 22	142		
1 Samuel 24	57		
2 Samuel 12	51		
2 Samuel 15	3		

2. The heart that loves God is a heart that bursts forth in songs of praise. Sing aloud a psalm or praise song.

Taproot

1. Doing God's will sometimes means we must wait patiently on Him. Read Psalm 40:1-2. Notice the term *pit of destruction* or *pit of despair*. What is your "pit" situation? What is causing you heartache, grief, or disappointment?

2. How God can lift you up out of the pit?

8 | For Those Who Truly Love God

Let me suggest three observations of those who truly love God.

1. You who truly love the Lord have experienced His power to deliver, so your fears are gone. You could write your own chapter. You could sing your own song of praise. Your fears have been taken away. Perfect love casts out fear, doesn't it?

2. You who truly love God have received His peace and forgiveness, so your guilt has been relieved. And what a relief it is! You don't spend your days washing around in how wrong or how badly you feel. You have claimed His mercy. You're free of guilt.

3. You who truly love God have felt His presence through affliction and your faith has been strengthened. You're stronger now. You know what's happened in the process? You and your Lord have become close friends—so close that the relationship can't really be explained in human terms. You have linked yourself with the Almighty and you and He are in league together. You're walking together. And nothing breaks that fellowship. That's the way it is with God. He's on that basis with His children.

Playwright Moss Hart once recalled a childhood Christmas when his father took him shopping, hoping to buy the boy a present he would like. The two walked the New York streets, inspecting the merchandise displayed on scores of pushcarts. Hart's eyes, as a little boy, were drawn to chemistry sets and to printing presses. But the father, a very poor man, had less expensive things in mind.

Each time they would find something the boy wanted, the

father would ask the vendor's price, shake his head, and move on. Occasionally he would pick up a smaller, less expensive toy and try to attract his son's attention. But there was no meeting of the minds. Eventually they came to the end of the line of pushcarts without a purchase.

Hart writes:

> I heard [my father] jingle some coins in his pocket. In a flash I knew it all. He had gotten together about seventy-five cents to buy me a Christmas present, and he hadn't dared say so in case there was nothing to be had for so small a sum. As I looked up at him I saw a look of despair and disappointment in his eyes that brought me closer to him than I had ever been in my life.
>
> I wanted to throw my arms around him and say, "It doesn't matter . . . I understand. . . . This is better than a printing press . . . I love you." But instead we stood shivering beside each other for a moment—then turned away from the last two pushcarts and started silently back home . . . I didn't even take his hand on the way home, nor did he take mine. We were not on that basis. Nor did I ever tell him how close to him I felt that night—that for a little while the concrete wall between father and son had crumbled away and I knew that we were two lonely people struggling to reach each other.[1]

You need to know that God wants to be on that basis with us. God wants our arms around Him. God wants to hear us say, "I love You, Father. I trust You. Whatever You want to give me I accept. I need You. I cling to You. I walk with You. I adore You."

The better you get to know God, the more comfortable you will be with that kind of response. And you gain comfort in that kind of response, express it. Sing your songs. Lay your burdens on Him. Trust Him with all your heart and might. He'll be honored as you do that.

Extending Your Roots

Read the following situations and write down how you would help the people involved.

1. Bill, a twenty-year employee of a major corporation, received a lay-off notice. His job has been his life. Bill worked his way up to a good position and salary. Now, fear is affecting his work and home life.

How would you help Bill? Find Scriptures to support your actions or to share with Bill.

2. Betsy and her mother have had a "shaky" mother-daughter relationship for years. In recent years, Betsy refuses to go back home to see her mother. The differences in their life-styles make communication impossible. They have nothing in common. The phone rings and Betsy hears this message, "Your mother has cancer."

How would you help Betsy? Find Scriptures to support your actions and encourage Betsy.

3. You have drifted away from God's will for your life. Career and pleasure have replaced attending church and praying. You are driving your new sports car down the interstate. An out-of-control truck crashes into your car. Months of hospital care have caused you to reevaluate your life.

What have you learned?

 *Taproot*

Make a list of ways you love God.

The Lord Jesus Christ

9 | Mary's Little Lamb

History tells us that early in the nineteenth century the whole world was watching with bated breath the campaigns of Napoleon. There was talk everywhere of marches, invasions, battles, and bloodshed as the French dictator pushed his way through Europe. Babies were born during that time. But who had time to think about babies or to care about cradles and nurseries when the international scene was as tumultuous as it was? Nevertheless, between Trafalgar and Waterloo there stole into this world a veritable host of heroes whose lives were destined to shape all of humanity. But, again I ask, who had time to think about babies while Napoleon was on the move?

Well, someone should have.

Let's take the year 1809. Internationally, everyone was looking at Austria, because that was where blood was flowing freely. In one campaign after another that year, Napoleon was sweeping through Austria. Nobody cared about babies in 1809, but when you check the record, you realize the world was overlooking some terribly significant births.

Take, for example, William Gladstone. Gladstone was destined to become one of the finest statesmen that England ever produced. In that same year Alfred Tennyson was born to an obscure minister and his wife. Tennyson would one day greatly affect the literary world in a marked manner. Oliver Wendell Holmes was born in Cambridge, Massachusetts, in 1809. And not far away in Boston, Edgar Allan Poe began his eventful, albeit tragic, life. It was also in that same year—1809—that a physician named Darwin and his wife named their child Charles Robert. And it was that same year that the cries of a newborn infant could be heard from a rugged log cabin in Hardin County, Kentucky. The baby's name? Abraham Lincoln.

If there had been news broadcasts at that time, I'm certain these words would have been heard: "The destiny of the world is being shaped on an Austrian battlefield today." Or was it?

Funny, only a handful of history buffs today could name even two or three of the Austrian campaigns. Looking back, you and I realize that history was actually being shaped in the cradles of England and America as young mothers held in their arms the shakers and the movers of the future. No one could deny that 1809 was, in fact, the genesis of an era.

The same could be said of the time when Jesus of Nazareth was born. No one in the entire Roman Empire could've cared less about the birth of that Jewish infant in Bethlehem. Rome ruled the world. *That's* where history was being made! Or was it?

Dr. Luke was as careful with his study of history as he was with his practice of medicine. In the Gospel that bears his name, he provides for us several dependable, helpful facts. We can look up these facts and realize that if never before, at least at that time, God chose things that seemed to be terribly insignificant to put to shame the things that seemed highly important. We'll be studying several things about Jesus as we continue thinking about the Trinity.

Root Issues

1. Luke 2 and Matthew 1:18 to 2:23 may comprise "the greatest story ever told." Don't limit this magnificent account of Christmas Eve! It's too important, too encouraging to be put on the shelf as a "yearly tradition." Read one or both of these passages out loud—either to yourself or to

Mary's Little Lamb

your family. Reflect on what it meant for God to become a baby . . . and a Man. Come, let us adore Him—today!

2. If it is near the Christmas season as you read these words, carefully think about how you might make better use of these days when so many non-Christian men and women, boys and girls think about the Babe, a manger, and Bethlehem. How might you grasp this special opportunity to introduce neighbors and relatives to Mary's Lamb—the One who was born to die for *all* the sins of *all* mankind? Could you compose a Christmas letter that includes a clear testimony of your faith—or perhaps the simple plan of salvation? How about an "open house" when you could invite in the neighbors for casual conversation and Christmas goodies? (It might open a door for you to speak about your Lord at some future time.) Groups such as SEARCH Ministries offer many creative and practical suggestions for planning such informal gatherings.

3. The headlines of today's newspaper and the covers of *Time* and *Newsweek* trumpet what the world considers the "major news" of the day. Actually, what transpires between you and your neighbor or you and your associate at work could have much deeper *eternal* significance. How long has it been since you actually prayed that the Lord would give you the privilege of speaking to someone about your Savior? "You shall be My witnesses," He tells us in Acts 1:8. A witness simply reports what he or she has seen and experienced—doesn't have to be a "sermon" or a dump truck load of information. Just a word at the right time about the greatest Hope in all the world. The *big* news is the good news. Write down your prayer request in your notebook and date it.

 *Extending Your Roots*

1. Bible students need a view of several important places

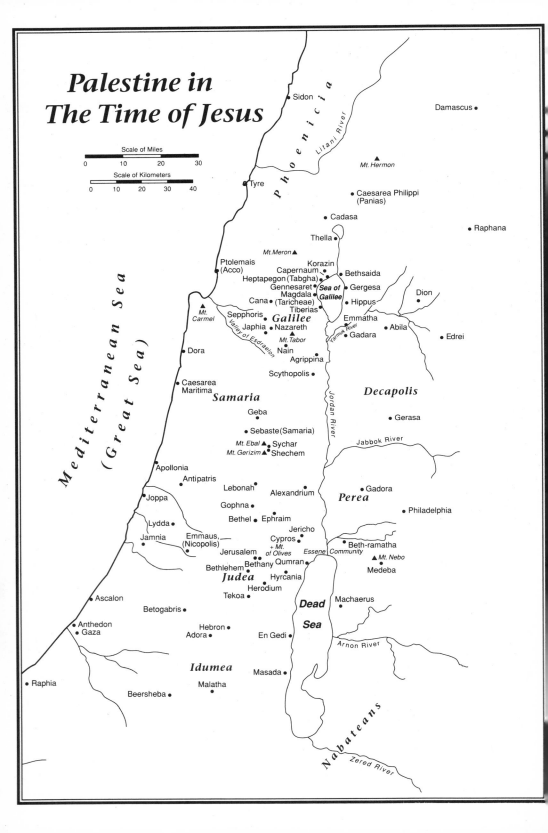

Mary's Little Lamb

in Mary and Joseph's world. On the map, identify these locations. Refer to a Bible atlas for assistance.

Capernaum
Bethany
Jerusalem
Sychar
Sea of Galilee
Dead Sea
Jericho
Jordan River
Bethlehem
Nazareth
Cana

2. Using an atlas or Bible dictionary, write a brief description of each place.

 *Taproot*

1. In an encyclopedia or Bible dictionary, read about the Roman Empire during this period of time. Why did Rome play such an important part in New Testament history?

10 | The Background Behind Jesus' Birth

> Now it came about in those days that a decree went out from Caesar Augustus, that a census be taken of all the inhabited earth (Luke 2:1).

To what days does Luke refer? What was the scene? It wasn't Napoleon in Austria, it was Caesar. And it wasn't only Caesar, it was all of Rome in all her power and splendor. The Roman Empire had stretched its real estate to maximum proportions. Its western boundary was the Atlantic Ocean. Its eastern boundary was the Euphrates. It reached as far north as the Danube and the Rhine and as far south as the Sahara desert. And there was one name prominent and paramount over all of this land. The caesar. His name was Augustus.

Now in the midst of this great, powerful structure known as the Roman Empire there was a little finger of land that struggled for existence and identity along the easternmost shores of the Mediterranean—the land of Palestine. But somehow God had graciously provided its security through the years—even to this day that is true. There had been raised from lowly birth a young man who came to be known as Herod the Great. He had been given tacit approval by Caesar Augustus to give a measure of guidance over the Jewish people in the land of Palestine, specifically, for our interest, Judea.

At the time of Herod the Great's death, he wrote a will that was, for the most part, honored by Caesar. Herod's territory would be given to his three sons. One was named Archelaus, a brutal tyrant. Archelaus would get Judea. He was anti-Semitic from the crown of his head to the soles of his feet. And for a decade—ten uninterrupted years—he ruled over the Jews with an iron fist until, finally, so many complaints came to the attention of Augustus that he banished Archelaus to Gaul, where he died in disgrace.

At that same time Augustus put his approval on a young man named Publius Quirinius, who lived in Syria serving as its president or governor (to use the words of Luke). And Quirinius, though unfamiliar with Judea, was brought to the land of Judea to change things around. In other words, Caesar was designing a plan to put into operation the machinery that would make Judea a Roman province for the first time. In order to do this he had to take care of two things: (1) He had to move the power structure (the power of life and death was taken out of the hands of the Jews and placed into the hands of Rome), and (2) he had to tax the people heavily to get them in line with the rest of the empire.

Those two things, it seemed to the world, were most unfair, and of maximum significance. But looking back, how insignificant they really were. The significant event was the birth of a baby in Bethlehem, but who could care about a baby born in Judea during a time when Caesar was expanding his kingdom? Who could care about a crying little infant when taxation was being increased?

And for the first time the Jews had no direct representative in Rome. At this juncture, it seems fitting that we leave Luke 2 and listen to a prophet's prediction for a moment. His name was Micah. I smile when I write that name because Micah was not even known by the Roman caesar. It is doubtful that he had even a passing interest in the writings of that obscure Jewish prophet. But Micah's prediction, written eight hundred years (did you get that?—eight centuries) before Caesar made his taxation decree, before he'd announced, "Archelaus, be gone! Quirinius, move in! Let's tax the world!" was about to be fulfilled. Caesar's decree made it necessary for a Jewish couple living in Nazareth to make a rugged eighty-mile journey from Nazareth to Bethlehem for the purpose of signing that taxation census. Participating in such a census required that a man go back to what, today, we would call his family "county seat." Now look back to Micah 5:2:

> But as for you, Bethlehem Ephrathah, Too little to be among the clans of Judah, From you One will go forth for Me to be ruler in Israel. His goings forth are from long ago, From the days of eternity.

Beth-le-hem means "house of bread" in Hebrew. Insignificant as a tiny loaf of bread, yet the Lord through the writing of a minor prophet eight centuries earlier puts his finger on Bethlehem and announces that this place will be famous. Why, that's like the President addressing Muleshoe, Texas, or Pea Ridge, Arkansas, saying, "From you there will come forth a great person." In fact, it seems so insignificant that for centuries men questioned the writings of Micah. How could it be that Bethlehem, "the house of bread," insignificant as a grain of wheat, would be the seed plot—the birthplace of one who

> . . . will arise and shepherd His flock. . . . And . . . be our peace (vv. 4-5).

You see, no one cared about the writings of Micah. I can picture pompous Augustus sitting securely on his throne, in charge of the Roman world, thinking he had made a decision that was altogether original and unique. But looking back, we realize he was running the errands of a minor prophet named Micah. Augustus had no earthly idea that a teenaged pregnant girl named Mary living in Nazareth with Joseph, her carpenter husband, was about to bear a son named Jesus, who would be the Savior of the world. But the world was about to find out that infant named Jesus was really the significance of that era, not Caesar. The spotlight of redemption's history would fall on Bethlehem, not Rome.

Luke tells us:

> . . . that a decree went out from Caesar Augustus, that a census be taken of all the inhabited earth. This was the first

census taken while Quirinius [there's our man] was governor of Syria (2:1-2).

So Quirinius cranked up the machinery that would put taxation into motion. I'm sure he went about his duties in a matter-of-fact fashion, knowing absolutely nothing of Micah's prophecy. As the dominoes began to bump up against one another, it became necessary for Mary and Joseph to travel from Nazareth to Bethlehem.

> And all were proceeding to register for the census, everyone in his own city (v. 3).

It looked like history was being made in the magnificent house of Caesar, but in actuality it was soon to be made in the lowly house of bread.

A capable journalist-author named Jim Bishop wrote a fairly reliable analysis of Jesus' birth in his book, *The Day Christ Was Born*. His description of Mary, the young mother-to-be, bears repeating:

> She no longer noticed the chafe of the goatskin against her leg, nor the sway of the food bag on the other side of the animal. Her veiled head hung and she saw millions of pebbles on the road moving by her brown eyes in a blur, pausing, and moving by again with each step of the animal.
>
> Sometimes she felt ill at ease and fatigued, but she swallowed this feeling and concentrated on what a beautiful baby she was about to have and kept thinking about it, the bathing, the oils, the feeding, the tender pressing of the tiny body against her breast—and the sickness went away. Sometimes she murmured the ancient prayers and, for the moment, there was no road and no pebbles and she dwelt on the wonder of God and saw Him in a fleecy cloud at a windowless wall of an inn or a hummock of trees, walking backward in front of her husband, beckoning him on. God was everywhere. It gave Mary confidence to know that He was everywhere. She needed confidence. Mary was fifteen.
>
> Most young ladies of the country were betrothed at thirteen and married at fourteen. A few were not joined in holiness until fifteen or sixteen and these seldom found a choice man and were content to be shepherds' wives, living in caves

in the sides of the hills, raising their children in loneliness, knowing only the great stars of the night lifting over the hills, and the whistle of the shepherd as he turned to lead his flock to a new pasture. Mary had married a carpenter. He had been apprenticed by his father at bar mitzvah. Now he was nineteen and had his own business.

It wasn't much of a business, even for the Galilean country. He was young and, even though he was earnest to the point of being humorless, he was untried and was prone to mistakes in his calculations. In all of Judea there was little lumber. Some stately cedars grew in the powdery alkaline soil, but, other than date palms and fig trees and some fruit orchards, it was a bald, hilly country. Carpentry was a poor choice.[1]

The story in Luke proceeds:

And Joseph also went up from Galilee, from the city of Nazareth, to Judea, to the city of David, . . . in order to register, along with Mary, who was engaged to him, and was with child (vv. 4-5).

If we could step into the time tunnel and return to those days, Luke's papers would be laid aside as rather bland and insignificant. After all, it was taxation that was important, not the birth of some little baby. It would have seemed as insignificant as the birth of an Oliver Wendell Holmes, an Edgar Allan Poe, or an Abraham Lincoln when Napoleon took Austria. But looking back on the scene, *nothing* was more important than Mary and Joseph's journey to Bethlehem. Within days, Messiah would be born!

Extending Your Roots

The birth of Jesus and surrounding events are familiar to all of us—or are they?

Complete the following quiz without looking the answers up in your Bible.

1. The angel _____ made three announcements.

The Background Behind Jesus' Birth

2. Joseph was a _____ by trade.

3. Mary went to visit her cousin _____

4. The fact that Mary was a when Jesus was born is very important.

5. Mary and Joseph had traveled to Bethlehem because Caesar Augustus had ordered a _____ .

6. Jesus was born in a _____ .

7. Mary was _____ to Joseph.

8. _____ men) came from the East bringing gifts.

9. _____ were in the fields nearby.

10. had been assured by God that he would live to see the Messiah.

How did you do? Now, find the correct answers to the quiz in your Bible. Write down the Scripture reference for future studies.

Taproot

1. The time is 742-687 B.C. How did God use a minor prophet of the Old Testament to tell the good news about Mary's Lamb? Read Micah 5 and Luke 2.

2. Today—How does God use *me* to tell the good news about Mary's Lamb? List several ways.

11 The Scene in Bethlehem

As we continue our study about Jesus, it will help you to realize that at that time Bethlehem was a confusing jungle, a hubbub of people. Not only did this taxation move Mary and Joseph from their home in Nazareth, it moved hundreds, perhaps thousands, of others as well. And the little town wasn't set up with motels and hotels as we are today. The best they had was what was known as a *caravansary*. It was like an ancient bus depot—where weary travelers in caravans would move in, be refreshed for a brief period, and then move on. But even the caravansary was full.

They tried other areas, but they were also full. No signs swung brightly after dark, reading, "Travelers welcome here for the night." Historians tell us that it was possible that the travelers slept all over the street during this heavy taxation time.

That was the harsh scene that met them when they came into Bethlehem. In fact, in verse 7, it says with a great deal of emotion, "there was no room for them in the inn." No room—not a single place for Messiah to be born.

Have you ever traveled from one city to another, knowing no one at the place of your destination? Most people I know have. And the pain was only intensified when, upon arriving, you found no room.

I'll never forget when Cynthia and I moved in 1957 from Houston to San Francisco. We had heard about its being a beautiful, picturesque, romantic city. And we found it to be so, after awhile. But at first glance there was no room any-where to stay. We searched and searched for an apart-ment—*any* apartment. It took us over a week of constant searching, and that was pretty quick. The search can be a terribly depressing experience.

I think perhaps one of the most moving stories of no room, besides this one that Luke gives us, is the one that a pastor friend of mine tells of his beginning days in the pastorate in a city back East many years ago. He tells of the time when he moved with his family—his wife, a little baby, and a cou-ple of other small children. They had accepted the pastorate of a church in a city where they knew no one.

When they arrived it was *Halloween night*—Saturday night. He was to preach his first sermon to his new flock the next morning. You should hear him describe the scene when they arrived! "Every fool was in the streets of that city on Halloween night. What a place!" It seemed as though no one even knew this pastor and his family were coming. No plans had been made. No one met them. No open house. No warm reception. No provision for his family. Not even a room at a hotel for that first night. So he pulled up to a pay phone and dialed the number of the one name he had. The fellow answered with a startled surprise, "Oh, yes, you *are* coming . . . that's right." The man drove over to meet him and then took him and his family to an attic at an old aban-doned theater. If you can believe it, that's where he began his pastorate—wrinkled clothes, crying baby, bottles, for-mula, and makeshift beds in a theater attic. That's where he prepared his first sermon. Talk about having to overcome first impressions!

But it was far worse for Mary. She was now only minutes removed from delivery. Exhausted from the long journey, she came to Bethlehem, and there was not one place to stay except in an animal enclosure by an inn. But who cared about a baby? The whole talk around the city was the prob-lem of taxation and Caesar and Quirinius and Archelaus—and Herod, who started it all. And the crying of that little infant was another irritant in the ears of the people wanting sleep because they were bothered to be in that strange place. Nobody cared, and there was no room.

So she had her little baby all alone. Only Joseph was near.

The sheep corral, filthy as only an Eastern animal enclosure can be, reeked pungently with manure and urine accumulated across the seasons. Joseph cleared a corner just large enough for Mary to lie down. Birth pains had started. She writhed in agony on the ground. Joseph, in his inexperience and unknowing manly manner, did his best to reassure her. His own other tunic would be her bed, his rough saddlebag her pillow. Hay, straw, or other animal fodder was nonexistent. This was not hay- or grain-growing country. Stock barely survived by grazing on the sparse vegetation that sprang from the semidesert terrain around the town.

Mary moaned and groaned in the darkness of the sheep shelter. Joseph swept away the dust and dirt from a small space in one of the hand-hewn mangers carved from the soft limestone rock. It was covered with cobwebs and debris fallen from the rock ceiling. There, as best he could, he arranged a place where Mary could lay the newborn babe all bundled up in the swaddling clothes she had brought along.

There, alone, unaided, without strangers or friends to witness her ordeal in the darkness, Mary delivered her son. A more lowly or humble birth is impossible to imagine. It was the unpretentious entrance, the stage entrance of the Son of man—the Son of God, God very God in human guise and form—upon earth's stage.

In the dim darkness of the stable a new sound was heard. The infant cry of the newborn babe came clearly. For the first time Deity was articulated directly in sounds expressed through a human body. Those sounds brought cheer, comfort, and courage to Mary and Joseph. These peasant parents were the first of multiplied millions upon millions who in the centuries to follow would be cheered and comforted by the sounds that came from that Voice.

God is come. God is with His people. Immanuel.[1]

And she bundled Him in wrappings, little makeshift

The Scene in Bethlehem

clothes, and put Him in the manger—her firstborn—Mary's little Lamb.

Every mother reading these words can identify with Mary. Remember your firstborn? My wife tells me of the occasion when our first child was born. She was fully conscious. She said, "There is no feeling at all like the feeling when they have taken the baby and cut the cord, then laid him alongside you. In fact (referring to our firstborn), they laid him right across my tummy. He stretched out, and I reached down and felt him. I thought, *Oh, dear God, life from me!*"

Extending Your Roots

1. Write a brief description of this small village.

2. Rearrange these events to place them in their proper order.

_____ Lodging was unavailable.

_____ Augustus ordered a Roman census.

_____ A stable was located.

_____ Descendants of King David must be counted in Bethlehem.

_____ The village was overcrowded.

_____ Joseph and Mary arrived in Bethlehem.

3. Read or sing a Christmas song about Bethlehem.

Taproot

1. What is the significance of Ruth and Naomi returning to Bethlehem? (See Ruth 2.)

12 | Mary's Lamb

Joseph cleaned up from the birth and put that little tiny life into a rough feeding trough. Mary looked down and saw *God* by her side. But nobody cared. One poet wrote:

They all were looking for a King
To slay their foes and lift them *high*:
Thou cam'st a little baby thing
That made a woman cry.[1]

And another:

A baby's hands in Bethlehem
Were small and softly curled.
But held within their dimpled grasp
The hope of all the world.[2]

The most significant event of the centuries took place in an enclosed patio made into a stable in an insignificant "loaf-of-bread" city, Bethlehem. I wonder what Mary thought? Haven't you wondered that when you have read the story? Haven't you wondered what went through her mind as she saw that little one? The most significant thing that happened didn't happen in Caesar's court, Quirinius's palace, or among the plans of the Jewish zealots to overthrow Rome. The most significant thing happened in a manger. As Mary held that baby, I wonder if she thought about Isaiah's words? Surely she knew them.

Therefore the Lord Himself will give you a sign: Behold, a virgin will be with child and bear a son, and she will call His name Immanuel (Isa.7:14).

She was holding in her arms Immanuel—"God with us." Or maybe she remembered the angel who had visited her nine months earlier and said, "Do not be afraid" (Luke 1:30).

Just like the Lord, isn't it? You see, God doesn't make edicts like man does. The Caesar makes a decree—it is announced and the world jumps to attention. But God's first concern is the feeling of the one that will hear the message, so He says, "Don't be afraid, Mary. Something amazing is going to happen. Behold, not knowing a man, you will conceive in your womb. You will bear a Son, and you will call His name Jesus." A never-to-be-repeated event! A virgin will have a baby . . . even though most people will never believe it.

I wonder if God gave her a passing premonition of John the Baptizer, who, in years to come, would look at Jesus and point that prophetic finger in His direction and say, "Behold, the Lamb of God who takes away the sin of the world"? Yes, Mary had a little Lamb that night. And her precious little Lamb was destined for sacrifice.

I think the Lord seems to underscore this as Luke records for us those who heard the announcement. You notice He didn't send angels to Rome. He didn't send them to Judea or Syria, or to other places of honor and significance. He sent the angels to a group of lowly shepherds (v. 8) who were staying out in the fields, keeping watch over their flock by night.

What flock? If it is true what I read in preparing my thoughts for this chapter, this was a very significant flock of sheep kept near Bethlehem. These sheep were set aside, destined for sacrificial altars. These were "slaughter sheep." And what a perfect group to announce the message of the gospel to, to tell those who were watching the sheep, "The Lord has come!"

There was a tiny Lamb in Bethlehem who was destined for Golgotha's altar.

In fact, Luke's record reads:

Growing Deep in the Christian Life: The Trinity

> And in the same region there were some shepherds staying out in the fields, and keeping watch over their flock by night. And an angel of the Lord suddenly stood before them, and the glory of the Lord shone around them; and they were terribly frightened (2:8-9).

Have you ever pictured what that must have been like? Here were half-asleep shepherds out keeping a flock of little woolies in the field, just like any other night, then suddenly it was brighter than high noon.

The Old Testament uses a word several times that is called the *shekinah*, which seems to describe the light that flows from heaven, giving brilliance to the place where God is. That light filled the holy place of the tabernacle. It later filled the temple where God's presence could be felt before His Son came to earth—burning light—resplendent, blinding light—the same light perhaps that struck Paul blind. That night this same light fell upon those shepherds. They saw the light, and naturally they were afraid. They had no idea what was going to be announced.

What had they been talking about? Like everyone else, they were talking about taxes, the change of government, the increased Roman rule that would impact the Jews—what it would mean to their families, the loss of freedom, the helplessness they felt, the fear. Those were the issues of that day. Suddenly, without any warning, the Lord spoke through the voices of the angel:

> Do not be afraid; for behold, I bring you good news of a great joy which shall be for all the people; for today in the city of David there has been born for you a Savior, who is Christ the Lord" (vv. 10-11).

Extending Your Roots

1. Using a concordance or word study book, find out how and where the word *lamb* is used in the Bible.
Write down your findings.

2. Write your own definition of *lamb*.

3. How many times does the word refer to Mary's Lamb?

4. Which writers used the word?

5. Where in the Bible do you first read about "lambs"?

6. What has Mary's Lamb done for you?

 *Taproot*

1. After reading Revelation 5, complete the following statement: The Lamb is _____ .

2. Continue the description of the Lamb by reading Isaiah 53:71 and Peter 1:19

3. Refresh your memory about the Passover. Read Exodus 12. How does Mary's Lamb complete the Passover?

13 The Significance of the Insignificant

There is a small verse in the book of 1 Corinthians that is a fitting motto for all that we have read in these first eleven verses of Luke 2. It goes like this:

> But God has chosen the foolish things of the world to shame the wise, and God has chosen the weak things of the world to shame the things which are strong (1:27).

If I could add my own paraphrase, "And God has chosen the Lamb of Mary to bring to nothing the authority of Rome."

Things haven't changed much, have they? Every Christmas season the significance seems to get lost among the insignificant. How often have you heard from people on the street, behind the counters, or outside the church, of the wonderful yet simple story of Jesus Christ? If you have heard it once or twice, you are very rare. Apart from Christian friends, it is remarkable if you hear that the Christmas message is Jesus Christ—His virgin birth, His incarnation, His coming to this earth. Because, you see, our world continues to be caught in the web of insignificant things like busy commerce—the profit-and-loss issues of life.

And Christ? Well, who can worry too much about Him when history is being made at the cash register. Or is it?

One true story I read recently told of a commercial venture of one of the largest department stores in our nation. It proved to be disastrously unsuccessful. It was a doll in the form of the baby Jesus. It was advertised as being unbreakable, washable, and cuddly. It was packaged in straw with a satin crib and plastic surroundings, and appropriate biblical texts added here and there to make the scene complete.

It did not sell. The manager of one of the stores in the department chain panicked. He carried out a last-ditch promotion to get rid of those dolls. He brandished a huge sign outside his store that read:

JESUS CHRIST— MARKED DOWN 50% GET HIM WHILE YOU CAN

My friend, Jesus is God's Lamb, the Son of God. He didn't come to be packaged and offered for half price where, if you hurry, you can get Him. He came as very God. And the world in its tinsel and tarnish has just about ruined the picture. As in the days of Rome, our God is not panicked over the scene of America or other nations of the world. Are you wise enough to see the significant in the midst of the insignificant?

Has there been a time in your personal life when you have asked Christ Jesus to occupy your heart, as He once occupied the manger? Honestly now, does He have first place? The Lord Jesus Christ is available in the same form He has been for centuries—the Son of God who died for you, who paid the price for your sin, who was raised from the dead, who is living. If you will, by personal invitation, ask Jesus to become the Lord of your life; He will come in. In the solitude of this quiet moment, make room in your heart for the Lord Jesus. Set the book aside and tell Him you take Him . . . you give Him the place of honor and authority in your life. I invite you to do that now.

Wise men still seek Him, you know.

Extending Your Roots

The significance of the Christmas season seems to be lost among Santa, reindeer, tinsel, trees, and presents.

1. Plan a Christmas season that honors Jesus Christ. Focus on Jesus' birth each day of the month. Use decorations that are reminders of Mary's Lamb.

Taproot

1. List some teachings you know about the incarnation.

2. Now read what these verses teach about the incarnation. Do these verses challenge or confirm what you know?

John 1:1-14   Hebrews 2:14

Romans 1:2-5   1 John 1:1-3

Philippians 2:6-11   1 Timothy 3:16

3. Complete this sentence: I believe the incarnation means:_____

14 When the God-Man Walked Among Us

Who is Jesus Christ? You may be surprised to know that that question has continued to be asked ever since the first century when He walked on earth. His identity has never failed to create a stir. Who exactly is this Jesus? The answers have varied from demon to Deity.

It is imperative that we know the right answer. Otherwise, we do not know how to interpret what He has done. And if we are unable to interpret what He has done, we will never be able to give ourselves to Him as He invites us to do.

Who Is Jesus Christ?

Even during the days of Jesus' earthly pilgrimage, there were many opinions. Let's travel through Matthew's Gospel and find out how varied the opinions really were.

The Wise Men

We come first to a group of men called magi or, more popularly, the wise men. Jesus had been born in Bethlehem. The magi had seen the star, which prompted them to journey a long distance. Finally, they arrived at Jerusalem, anxious to discover His whereabouts.

> Now after Jesus was born in Bethlehem of Judea in the days of Herod the king, behold, magi from the east arrived in Jerusalem, saying, "Where is He who has been born King of the Jews? For we saw His star in the east, and have come to worship Him" (Matt. 2:1-2).

There was no question in their minds, the birth of Jesus represented the birth of a king. The star was "His star." Clearly in their minds, He was "King of the Jews," and they had come to bow down before Him in worship.

God the Father

At the age of thirty, Jesus was baptized by John in the Jordan River. Coming up out of the water, a voice broke through the clouds of heaven, announcing His identity:

> And after being baptized, Jesus went up immediately from the water; and behold, the heavens were opened, and He saw the Spirit of God descending as a dove, and coming upon Him, and behold, a voice out of the heavens, saying, "This is My beloved Son, in whom I am well-pleased" (3:16-17).

There was no question in God's mind. "I have given you My beloved Son."

Later, at what we know as the transfiguration, on a mountain with some of His disciples, the same voice spoke yet again, making the same announcement: "This is My beloved Son, with whom I am well-pleased; listen to Him" (17:5).

The wise men, along with God the Father, had no question. "He is the King of the Jews." "He is My Son." But when it came to people on earth, in the milieu of everyday life, there were many who did not agree. Let's hear from several of them.

The Pharisees

The best that the Pharisees ever said of Him was that He was a teacher, a rabbi.

> And it happened that as He was reclining at table in the house, behold many tax-gatherers and sinners came and were dining with Jesus and His disciples. And when the Pharisees saw this, they said to His disciples, "Why is your Teacher eating with the tax-gatherers and sinners?" (9:10-11).

That was, no doubt, the most respectable title they ever

used for Jesus—"Teacher." They realized He instructed His followers, He spent time discussing spiritual things. At best, they viewed Him as "Teacher."

But things degenerated quickly for the Pharisees. That same group of men later said, "He casts out the demons by the ruler of the demons" (v. 34). In other words, "He represents the enemy. His power comes from the pit—from hell itself."

You may be surprised to know that not all of those who were confused over Jesus' identity could be listed among what we would call His enemies.

John the Baptizer

Many people are very surprised when they discover that the one who baptized Christ became so despondent and disillusioned that he questioned His identity—yes, John—John the Baptizer!

> Now when John in prison heard of the works of Christ, he sent word by his disciples, and said to Him, "Are You the Expected One, or shall we look for someone else?" (11:2-3).

I find that rather startling. Here is the same man who baptized Him. Here is the forerunner—the one who had paved the way for His arrival, who earlier declared: "Behold, the Lamb of God who takes away the sin of the world!" (John 1:29). This was John, the humble prophet who admitted that Jesus was the Christ, saying, "the thong of whose sandal I am not worthy to untie" v. 27). This was the same John who, having compared himself to Jesus, had said, "He must increase, but I must decrease" (3:30).

But things have changed. He is now saying that he has serious doubts. With severe concern John asked, "Are You the Expected One, or shall we look for someone else?" (v. 3). In other words, "I don't know who You are. Your works don't seem to square with the things that You're supposed to do as Messiah. I'm beginning to wonder myself—just who are You?"

Jesus' Neighbors and Immediate Family

If that isn't strange enough, consider Jesus' own family and friends in the neighborhood where He was raised. This scene is captured in Matthew 13.

> And it came about that when Jesus had finished these parables, He departed from there. And coming to His home He began teaching them in their synagogue, so that they became astonished, and said, "Where did this man get this wisdom, and these miraculous powers? Is not this the carpenter's son? Is not His mother called Mary, and His brothers, James and Joseph and Simon and Judas? And His sisters, are they not all with us? Where then did this man get all these things?" And they took offense at Him (13:53-57).

That certainly puts the knife to the fallacious doctrine of the perpetual virginity of Mary. Matthew's record assures us that Mary had other children. He even records a few names. Jesus was the firstborn, of course, but His neighbors were unconvinced that He was anything special. The neighbors, in effect, were asking: "Isn't this the kid my kids were raised with? Isn't He the one who, years ago, played hide 'n seek with them around the corner? Isn't this the same One we saw grow up in His father's carpenter shop? Isn't He the One who repaired our cabinet? He's the same Jesus, isn't He? Where in the world did He get these miraculous powers? Why does everybody applaud and respect Him? He's just one of us!"

They were confused. "Where did he get all these things?" Verse 57 says, "They took offense at Him."

"How dare You call Yourself the Son of God. You're just the son of Joseph!"

If that doesn't surprise you, just take a quick glance at Mark, chapter 3. I want you to zero in on His immediate family. It's bad enough to come home and be a prophet without honor, but to return to His own family and to hear them question His authority would be insult added to injury. Yet that is precisely what happened.

And he came home, and the multitude gathered again, to such an extent that they could not even eat a meal (v. 20).

Now watch:

And when His own people heard of this, they went out to take custody of Him; for they were saying, "He has lost His senses" (v. 21).

Tell me, were you aware that there was a time in Jesus' earthly life when His own flesh and blood considered Him insane?

Herod the Tetrarch

One of the officials in Jesus' day feared that He was John the Baptizer, risen from the dead.

At that time Herod the tetrarch heard the news about Jesus, and said to his servants, "This is John the Baptist; he has risen from the dead" (Matt.14:1-2).

Herod was haunted by thoughts of John, because John had been the one who had said to him earlier, "You're living in sin," while Herod was living with his brother's wife. John is the one whose head Herod required after watching Salome dance. And when word reached him about Jesus, he thought, *Oh no, the ghost of John has come to haunt me. This isn't Jesus—this must be John the Baptizer raised from the dead!"* Almost like Edgar Allan Poe's moving short story, "The Tell-Tale Heart" (which still sends chills up my back). The murderer thinks he hears the heartbeat of the man he had murdered and buried in the basement . . . thump . . . thump . . . thump . . . thump . . . thump. That pumping heart haunts him. In actuality it is his own heart. That's what Herod was living with: "This isn't any Messiah. This is John, back from beyond. I can't escape him."

The General Public's Opinion

Jesus later dialogued with His disciples, asking about His identity. The disciples, I think, rather calmly yawned and said:

[Oh,] . . . Some say John the Baptist; and others, Elijah; but still others, Jeremiah, or one of the prophets (16:14).

This casual conversation occurred in a brief moment. Matthew slips this information in to show us more evidence that when it came to Jesus' identity, many folks didn't have a clue.

What a mixture! Here's Herod saying, "He's John raised from the dead." Here's John the Baptizer in prison, bewildered and impatient, asking, "Are You really the Coming One?" Earlier there were magi, saying, "He's the King of the Jews." God the Father, saying, "My beloved Son." And now a group of people are saying, "Oh, He's Elijah . . . He's Jeremiah . . . He's one of the prophets back from beyond." Interestingly, some people actually agreed with Herod. "You really must be John," they were saying.

Peter, the Disciple

That same conversation continues:

He said to them, "But who do you say that I am?" And Simon Peter answered and said, "Thou art the Christ, the Son of the living God" (vv. 15-16).

This was one of Peter's greatest moments. He could not have been more correct.

The Citizens in Jerusalem

You might think that most of the people in the city would know that Jesus was Messiah; certainly they would as He entered the city on the back of a donkey, fulfilling prophecy. But they didn't. Even at His triumphal entry, there was a group of people who had no idea who He was.

And when He had entered Jerusalem, all the city was stirred, saying, "Who is this?" And the multitudes were saying, "This is the prophet Jesus, from Nazareth in Galilee" (21:10-11).

There were a few who cried, "Hosanna to the Son of David. Blessed is He who comes in the name of the Lord. Hosanna in the highest!" (v. 9), quoting from the psalmist. But there were many who stood back, scratching their bearded faces and saying, "We don't have any idea who that man is. I don't even know who He thinks He is. Honestly, I don't know."

Caiaphas, the High Priest

After being betrayed by Judas, Jesus was placed on trial. Not one trial, but six trials. All of them kangaroo courts. The most farcical series of trials in the history of jurisprudence were the trials of Jesus—every one illegal. He was brought to a man named Caiaphas, who was the high priest. And Caiaphas, looking into His eyes, pressed Him for His identity.

> But Jesus kept silent. And the high priest said to Him, "I adjure You by the living God, that You tell us whether You are the Christ, the Son of God" (26:63).

Christ means "Anointed One." When reading the Bible you can always think *Messiah* when you come to the word *Christ.*

"Tell us whether You are the Anointed One, the Son of God," the priest demanded. "We don't know who You are. We heard who You claimed to be. You tell us."

> Jesus said to him, "You have said it yourself; nevertheless I tell you, hereafter you shall see the Son of Man sitting at the right hand of Power, and coming on the clouds of heaven." Then the high priest tore his robes, saying, "He has blasphemed! What further need do we have of witnesses? Behold, you have now heard the blasphemy; what do you think?" They answered and said, "He is deserving of death!" Then they spat in His face and beat Him with their fists; and others slapped Him, and said, "Prophesy to us, You Christ; who is the one who hit You?" (vv. 64-68).

After such hostile indignities, they hustled Him off to Pilate.

Growing Deep in the Christian Life: The Trinity

Pilate

Now Pilate was an interesting study. He was in a Catch-22 situation. He was already suspect in the eyes of the Romans. And he was so anti-Semitic that he was hated by the Jews. So much so that there had been more than one insurrection against his rulership as a governor of Judea. So he was in hot water. When it came to Jesus, Pilate couldn't win.

So the Jewish officials pushed Jesus before Pilate. He was forced to deal with the identity of this man who claimed He was the Son of God (which meant nothing to him as a Roman since he had many gods). So he had to interpret the problem through their ears and eyes. And he couldn't ignore them. If he did there would be another insurrection and he'd be gone. But, you see, they needed Roman authority to put Jesus to death, because the Jews couldn't perform capital punishment; that was strictly a Roman act. So they were forced to plead their cause through Pilate. He didn't want to deal with it, but he had to.

> Now Jesus stood before the governor, and the governor questioned Him, saying, "Are You the King of the Jews?" And Jesus said to him, "It is as you say" (27:11).

Hold your place and go now to John's Gospel. The same question, the same interrogation, is recorded here in chapter 18:

> Pilate therefore entered again into the Praetorium, and summoned Jesus, and said to Him, "You are the King of the Jews?" Jesus answered, "Are you saying this on your own initiative, or did others tell you about Me?" Pilate answered, "I am not a Jew, am I? Your own nation and the chief priests delivered You up to me: what have You done?" Jesus answered, "My kingdom is not of this world. If My kingdom were of this world, then My servants would be fighting, that I might not be delivered up to the Jews, but as it is, My kingdom is not of this realm." Pilate therefore said to Him, "So You are a king?" Jesus answered, "You say correctly that I am a king. For this I have been born, and for this I have come

into the world, to bear witness to the truth. Every one who is of the truth hears My voice." Pilate said to Him, "What is truth?" (vv. 33-38).

So Pilate, in good Shakespearean fashion, finally washed his hands of the thing. "I'll have nothing to do with Him. You take Him and do with Him as you please. I find no fault in Him." With that, they prepared Jesus for the cross. Even though Pilate was convinced of Jesus' innocence, he lacked the courage to stand by his convictions.

They painted a sign. It was the custom in those days to put a sign on the top of a criminal's cross. Much like you would know the reason a person would go to the gas chamber or an electric chair. In those days the reason was spelled out so that all who passed by could read it, for capital punishment was done in a public place so as to deter further crimes. Jesus' sign was painted, according to John 19:19:

JESUS THE NAZARENE, THE KING OF THE JEWS

Now that's what Pilate wanted to appear on the sign to be nailed on Jesus' cross. But the Jewish officials said, "Wha . . . wh . . . we don't want that! No!" When the Jews read it, they saw it was done in Hebrew, Latin, and Greek. But they disapproved of the wording.

> And so the chief priests of the Jews were saying to Pilate, "Do not write, 'The King of the Jews'; but that He said, 'I am King of the Jews' " (v. 21).

"There's a lot of difference," the priests were saying. "When you put that sign on the cross, you're making a statement— 'He is.' We want everybody who passes by to know this is what He claimed, but that is definitely not what He was. He was not our king." The One the magi had pursued, because they viewed Him as a king, was crucified because the people refused to believe He was a king. What an irony!

Jesus Himself

When you get to Luke 24, Jesus has gone to death and beyond. He's come out of the grave. He has victoriously risen in bodily form, and He is speaking to His disciples. I find it most intriguing that in verse 44, Jesus goes back into the Old Testament and mentions words out of the Old Testament, words concerning Himself.

> Now He said to them, "These are My words which I spoke to you while I was still with you, that all things which are written about Me in the Law of Moses and the Prophets and the Psalms must be fulfilled."

This is one of the few times Jesus took people through the Scriptures and explained Himself to them from the Law, from the Psalms, and from the Prophets. "You see that? That was a reference to Me. You see this? That's spoken of Me. You see what the prophet said? I fulfill this."

> Then He opened their minds to understand the Scriptures, and He said to them, "Thus it is written, that the Christ should suffer and rise again from the dead the third day; and that repentance for forgiveness of sins should be proclaimed in His name to all the nations, beginning from Jerusalem. You are witnesses of these things (vv. 45-48).

"Men, you have had a unique privilege—to have lived during transition. You've seen Me carry these things out. Now I've come back from the grave. And I'm declaring to you, 'This is truth. I am who I claim to be, undiminished deity, true humanity, and in one person.'"

Or as John write, "The Word became flesh, and dwelt among us." The word *"dwelt"* is the word for "tabernacled" or "pitched a tent." I've heard the verse paraphrased, "The Word became flesh and pitched His tent among us for thirty-three years." And John, the disciple, testified:

> and we beheld His glory, glory as of the only begotten from the Father, full of grace and truth. John bore witness of Him, and cried out, saying, "This was He of whom I said, 'He who

comes after me has a higher rank than I, for He existed before me.' " For of His fulness we have all received, and grace upon grace (John 1:14-16).

"The Word became flesh. God became man. And as man, He lives among us, and we give Him glory. No question, He is the Son of God."

C. S. Lewis puts his finger on the real issue:

> I am trying here to prevent anyone saying the really foolish thing that people often say about Him: "I'm ready to accept Jesus as a great moral teacher, but I don't accept His claim to be God." That is the one thing we must not say. A man who was merely a man and said the sort of things Jesus said would not be a great moral teacher. He would either be a lunatic—on a level with the man who says he is a poached egg—or else he would be the Devil of Hell. You must make your choice. Either this man was, and is, the Son of God: or else a madman or something worse. You can shut Him up for a fool, you can spit at Him and kill Him as a demon; or you can fall at His feet and call Him Lord and God. But let us not come with any patronizing nonsense about His being a great human teacher. He has not left that open to us. He did not intend to.[1]

Here you are, sitting and reading this information—perhaps realizing for the first time that the evidence is undeniable. Or you may be thinking, "Mmmm, OK, Chuck, you've at least gotten my attention. I can see enough by what you've written that they were confused, yet I need more evidence to be convinced." So for your sake, in the next chapter I want to take one example from each of the four Gospels where Jesus Christ revealed Himself as both God and man.

 *Root Issues*

1. Review Matthew 13:53-57 and Mark 3:20-21. Jesus knew what it meant to be misunderstood by friends and family. Have you experienced the pain of being misunderstood recently? What clues can you find in 1 Peter 2:18-23

about our Lord's response to unfair treatment? Look a little further on in 1 Peter 3:8-18 for even more encouragement!

2. Memorize Hebrews 1:3 and John 1:1-3 and/or John 14:9 so that you will have an answer for those you meet who say, "Jesus may have been a great teacher—but He wasn't God." When someone says, "Well, who do *you* say He is?" be ready with an reply!

3. Reread Matthew 14:22-33. This time, *put yourself there*. This is no fairy tale—it really happened. Do your best to visualize the whole scene in vivid detail . . . the surging waves, that eerie night, the sight of a figure in the distance walking on the water. As soon as you have the opportunity, tell that story to a child to help that little one understand "who He really is." (TOTALLY AWESOME.) Or, visualize a similar scene in Luke 8:22-25. This time describe to an adult how Jesus—as God!—specializes in calming the waves and winds that come into your life.

Extending Your Roots

1. Let's take a look back through Jesus' earthly life and see who He said He was.

John 10:34-36 _____

Matthew 8:20 _____

Mark 3:11-12 _____

Luke 24:25-27 _____

John 13:13-14 _____

Mark 2:1-12 _____

Taproot

Tips for learning about a Bible character:

(1) Select the biblical person to be studied.

(2) Make a list of all references about the person.

When the God-Man Walked Among Us

(3) Write down some basic observations and important information.

(4) Develop a chronological outline of events.

(5) Select some helpful insights into the character of the person.

(6) Examine the person's life for illustrations of other biblical truths.

1. Stop here and prepare a biographical study of Jesus Christ. This is a big topic, so you may want to use the following outline to guide your study.

- From His birth to His baptism
- His temptations and early Judean ministry
- His ministry in Galilee
- The four separate journeys outside Galilee
- The period of His last journey
- The last week and crucifixion
- His resurrection, appearances, and ascension.

2. After completing the outline, answer this question: Who exactly is this Jesus?

3. What have you learned in your study that you can apply to your life this week?

15 Examples of Humanity and Deity

I want to mention four examples in which Jesus demonstrated His humanity—then immediately on the heels of that displayed His Deity. Maybe you've never made such a study. Let's limit it to one per Gospel writer.

> And immediately He made the disciples get into the boat, and go ahead of Him to the other side, while He sent the multitudes away. And after He had sent the multitudes away, He went up to the mountain by Himself to pray (Matt. 14 :22-23*a*).

We see Jesus' humanity as we find Him in prayer. You will never read of a place recorded in Scripture where God prays. Deity has no needs. Prayer is an act of mankind. Humans pray. Prayer is an expression of need. It is a declaration of adoration. God adores no one. There is no one higher to adore. He is self-contained, self-sufficient. All glory resides in Him. But humans pray because of an expression of a need to worship, to ask for strength, to request assistance, guidance, or whatever. And that's what Jesus is doing. In praying He shows himself human. His Deity is displayed in the next scene:

> and when it was evening, He was there alone. But the boat was already many stadia away from the land, battered by the waves; for the wind was contrary. And in the fourth watch of the night He came to them, walking upon the sea (14:23*b*-25).

It seemed to the disciples that Jesus came out of nowhere,

walking toward them on the water. And they looked across the sea and saw Him coming and they were scared to death. They screamed: "*Phantasma! Phantasma!*" That's the word Matthew uses. It is from that word we get our word *fantasy* or *fantastic* or *phantom*. It's as if they yelled, "It's an apparition! It's a ghost! Look!"

And so naturally Peter says, "If that's the Lord walking on the water, I'm going to try it, too!" So he stumbles out into the water, and he soon goes under. He can't pull it off. Later, a very significant conversion occurred:

> And when they got into the boat [both of them—one was wet and the other one dry, I might add], the wind stopped. [That in itself is remarkable!] And those who were in the boat worshiped Him, saying, "You [singular] are certainly God's Son!" (vv. 32-33).

Only man prays. Only God walks on water. According to Matthew, Jesus Christ did both.

Mark records another occasion where humanity and Deity were seen together.

> And a leper came to Him, beseeching Him and falling on his knees before Him, and saying to Him, "If You are willing, You can make me clean" (Mark 1:40).

I don't know if you've ever seen leprosy. I have. While in the Orient during my days in the Marine Corps, it was customary for my military outfit to visit a leprosarium once or twice a year. We went to entertain and encourage them. I have never seen such helpless, tragic sights. The hands and feet of those poor folk are oftentimes just bleeding stumps. No shoes of any kind can be worn, and it's obvious some of them don't even have feet or toes.

I can imagine this tragic man, with his bleeding stumps, saying to Jesus, "If You're willing, cleanse me."

Scripture never speaks of leprosy being cured or healed— always cleansed, because leprosy is the biblical picture of sin. We are never cured or healed of sin. We're cleansed of it. The leper says, "You can do it. Ah, I know You can heal me if You're willing. I know You can cleanse me." That's the word he used. "You can make me clean!"

As a man, the Lord Jesus is moved with compassion over a fellow human being in need. Years ago the original *King James Version* spoke of one being moved "deep within his own bowels of mercies." It's the best expression the Elizabethan English had of that pit of the stomach where you churn. One writer calls it our "churning place." He churned down deep (if I may) in His "gut." Men do that. Women do that. When you walk by a scene that is tragic, when you view one on the television screen, or read of one in a magazine or a newspaper, you are moved with compassion. That's human mercy expressed over human misery. That's an example of Jesus' humanity. But He doesn't stop with just humanity.

> And moved with compassion, He stretched out His hand and touched him, and said to him, "I am willing; be cleansed." And immediately the leprosy left him and he was cleansed (vv. 41-42).

Only God can do that. For all we know there were suddenly toes on the feet, fingers on the hands. The ache ended; the hemorrhaging stopped. And God in man had done His work.

Another great story occurred on the sea, according to Dr. Luke.

> Now it came about on one of those days, that He and His disciples got into a boat, and He said to them, "Let us go over to the other side of the lake." And they launched out. But as they were sailing along He fell asleep (8:22-23*a*).

I've not done a great deal of sailing, but the little sailing I've done, I've usually fallen asleep. It's the most natural response to the rhythm of the sea as it massages the weariness of my bones. Most humans I know would agree—easygoing sailing and restful sleeping are meant for each other! But, in Scripture, it's never said that God sleeps. In fact, it specifically says, "He who keeps Israel Will neither slumber nor sleep" (Ps. 121:4). Yet man sleeps. Humanity must sleep.

Examples of Humanity and Deity

Here, as a man, weary from the day, according to this passage, He falls sound asleep in the boat. That's when things started to happen:

> and a fierce gale of wind descended upon the lake, and they began to be swamped and to be in danger. And they came to Him and woke Him up, saying, "Master, Master, we are perishing!" (vv. 23b-24a)

"Master, wake up, wake up! We're gonna die!" Now isn't that something?

They've already witnessed the feeding of the five thousand. And each had a basket of food left over, but they hadn't learned the lesson of His power.

They'd seen Him walk on water and cleanse a leper . . . but they hadn't connected either with His Deity.

So here they are in a boat with God in flesh, and they say, "We're gonna sink." You can't sink with God on the same boat! And suddenly, with a word, everything is calm. Only God could do such a thing!

> And being aroused, He rebuked the wind and the surging waves, and they stopped, and it became calm (v. 24b).

I may not have done much sailing, but I have certainly done a lot of fishing in my day, and I can tell you I have occasionally seen the sea become what we fishermen usually call "a slick." It's an eerie sight—especially in the ocean. The water is so smooth that if you flipped a penny into it you could count the ripples. But never in my life have I seen a slick occur suddenly. Yet in this case a storming, raging, sea—with incredible wind velocity—instantly became a slick. You could hear your own breath. Their boat may have taken a few minutes to stop rocking, but the sea was calm as glass.

Look again at the disciples' response. It's great.

> And they were fearful and amazed [they spent half their lives fearful and amazed, didn't they?], saying to one another, "Who then is this, that He commands even the winds and the water, and they obey Him?" (v. 25).

Doesn't that sound like strong, believing followers? "Who is this?" Can't you see Peter, the fisherman, mumbling under his breath, "Even the winds and the waves obey Him." This is GOD. Yes, Peter, the One you woke up a moment ago is indeed God. HE IS GOD.

Never doubt it, my friend. In the tragic storms of life He specializes in calming waves and silencing winds. It'll just shock you sometimes. How can Jesus Christ do such a thing? He is God!

The last scene we want to relive has to do with Jesus' friend, Lazarus, who became ill and died shortly thereafter. Finally Jesus arrives on the scene of death. He meets up with blame since He hadn't dropped everything and earlier come alongside the grieving family. It's bad enough to be blamed.

> If you had been here, my brother would not have died (John 11:32).

But to face the grief of His friends—

> When Jesus therefore saw her weeping, and the Jews who came with her, also weeping, He was deeply moved in spirit, and was troubled (v. 33).

You'll never read of God's being troubled. Not like this. That's the human part of Jesus—humanity on display.

> "Where have you laid him?" They said to Him, "Lord, come and see." Jesus wept (vv. 34-35).

Neither will you read of God's weeping in the heavens. Tears are a human trait, not divine. He wept as He grieved, not only because of their unbelief, but over the loss of His friend and the sorrow of His companions. It was a scene where any one of us would cry.

> Jesus therefore again being deeply moved within, came to the tomb. Now it was a cave, and a stone was lying against it. Jesus said, "Remove the stone." Martha, the sister of the deceased, said to Him, "Lord, by this time there will be a stench; for he has been dead four days." Jesus said to her,

Examples of Humanity and Deity

"Did I not say to you, if you believe, you will see the glory of God?" (vv. 38-40).

You don't argue much with Jesus, you notice. Maybe one line. That's all. "I said, 'Move the stone.' " So they moved it.

Jesus, you see, is not going to resurrect Lazarus; He will resuscitate Him. If He would have resurrected Him, the stone could have stayed, because in the resurrection state the whole molecular structure of one's body changes and you can pass through wood, stone, glass, or space with no resistance. It's a whole different makeup. But you must move the stone out of the way if you are going to bring a man back from beyond and resuscitate him. So He says, "Move the stone."

> And so they removed the stone. And Jesus raised His eyes, and said, "Father, I thank Thee that Thou heardest Me. And I knew that Thou hearest Me always, but because of the people standing around I said it, that they may believe that Thou didst send Me." And when He had said these things, He cried out with a loud voice, "Lazarus, come forth" (vv. 41-43).

I love the country preacher's comment, "If He hadn't limited that command to Lazarus, every corpse in the graveyard would have come forth!" It was as if He said, "Just Lazarus, this time, just Lazarus." Some day He'll bring them all back!

A great scene follows. We've got a mummy staggering out of the tomb.

> He who had died came forth, bound hand and foot with wrappings; and his face was wrapped around with a cloth. Jesus said to them, "Unbind him, and let him go" (v. 44).

Isn't that an electric moment! Wouldn't you love to have had supper with Lazarus that night? "How was it, Lazarus?"

Only humans can weep in grief. And Jesus did. Only God can raise the dead. And Jesus did.

G. Campbell Morgan, when wrestling with the mystery of Christ's incarnation, once wrote:

He was the God-man. Not God indwelling a man. Of such there have been many. Not a man Deified. Of such there had been none save in the myths of pagan systems of thought; but God and man, combining in one Personality the two natures, a perpetual enigma and mystery, baffling the possibility of explanation.[1]

The apostle John's final comment in his Gospel goes like this:

This is the disciple who bears witness of these things, and wrote these things; and we know that his witness is true. And there are also many other things which Jesus did, which if they were written in detail, I suppose that even the world itself would not contain the books which were written (John 21:24-25).

It's as if John were saying, "I could have gathered up materials the world over and would not have had enough paper to write the stories with convincing, irrefutable evidence that He is who He claimed to be—namely, very God come in human form to die, to be raised, that you might see how magnificent He really is!"

Who is Jesus Christ? The God-man—the most unique Person who ever lived. The awesome Son of God!

Some time ago a lady wrote me a true story of an event that happened in a Christian school:

A kindergarten teacher was determining how much religious training her new students had. While talking with one little boy, to whom the story of Jesus was obviously brand new, she began relating His death on the cross. When asked what a cross was, she picked up some sticks, and fashioning a crude one, she explained that Jesus was actually nailed to that cross, and then He died. The little boy with eyes downcast quietly acknowledged, "Oh, that's too bad." In the very next breath, however, she related that He arose again and that He came back to life. And his little eyes got big as saucers. He lit up and exclaimed, "Totally awesome!"

You don't know the full identity of Jesus if your response

is "Oh, that's too bad." You know His identity only if your description is "TOTALLY AWESOME!"

Extending Your Roots

1. Fill in the statements below.

After feeding the five thousand (Matt. 14:22-23), Jesus went up into the mountains to pray. This is evidence of Jesus'_____.

A storm was endangering the disciples' boat. Jesus came to the rescue by _____, an evidence of His _____ .

The cleansing of the leper demonstrated Jesus' _____ .

2. Give two more examples of Jesus' humanity and Deity

3. Three of Jesus' followers claimed the Deity of Christ.

Read	*Who is speaking?*	*His Claim*
John 20:31		
Matthew 16:16		
John 20:28		

Now add your own claim. I believe Jesus is:

Taproot

1. In John, chapter 5, Jesus cites four proofs of His Deity. List the proofs.

2. Why do you believe Jesus was both divine and human?

16 Changing Lives Is Jesus' Business

It was Karl Marx, the father of modern socialism, who said, "Philosophers have only interpreted the world differently; the point is, however, to *change* it."

After serving the Lord for some fifteen years in Pakistan, missionary Warren Webster was invited to speak at the now famous Urbana Missionary Conference. He spoke very candidly about his days in Pakistan, but part of his message that his listeners will never forget are these words:

> If I had my life to live over again, I would live it to change the lives of people, because you have not changed anything until you have changed the lives of people.

Changing the world requires changing the lives of people.

While thinking through this chapter, I drifted back to the year 1973 and remembered the most famous musical our generation of Christians ever heard and sang. It's that immortal piece of music Bill and Gloria Gaither composed—*Alleluia, A Praise Gathering for Believers.* I thumbed through the musical and came across the part of the narration that mentions changing lives. The narrator breaks into the familiar melody, "Something beautiful, something good, all my confusion He understood . . ." with:

> Well, down through history, changing lives has been His business. He's changed the rich—changed the poor. He's changed the high and the mighty and He has changed the meek. He's changed my life, maybe He's changed yours. But if He hasn't, it can happen for you—right now! Today![1]

Marx, Webster, Gaither—talk about three unlikely bed-fellows! Yet a socialist, a missionary, and a Christian song-writing team agree at one point. They may be poles apart in philosophy and coming at the subject of change from different cultures, but all three agree, and we do too, that the key to changing our world is changing people. That is not optional, it is essential.

When I think about that which keeps me going in my ministry, it is the hope of *change*. When I meet with people who have struggled through the battles, the valleys, and the swamps of their experiences, and I search for reasons they hang on and keep growing, I discover that it is the hope of *change*. It is the inner conviction that God is at work, changing them and working through them to change others.

Just think about yourself for the last ten years. You're not the same person, are you? In fact, if you go back even further, and if you were completely candid, you'd have to admit that your life today compared to twelve, fifteen, eighteen years ago, doesn't even resemble the same person. Why? You are changing—and if it's for the better, I commend you!

Scriptural Statements
Regarding Changed Lives

Before we analyze three lives Jesus changed, let's take a brief look at the Old and New Testaments and trace the idea of change. We are going to discover that the concept was of major significance to the Lord our God. His specialty is changing people.

The Old Testament

Let's look first into the Book of Jeremiah, chapter 18. Glance over the first four verses from that chapter.

> The word which came to Jeremiah from the Lord saying, "Arise and go down to the potter's house, and there I shall announce My words to you." Then I went down to the potter's house, and there he was, making something on the wheel. But the vessel that he was making of clay was spoiled

in the hand of the potter; so he remade it into another vessel,
as it pleased the potter to make.

If you have never seen a potter at work, your education
isn't complete. You owe it to yourself to take the time to
observe an artist at work on the wheel. It's fascinating!

Several years ago my wife and I visited a local university
campus during their art festival. We had the privilege of
slipping behind the curtain and watching a potter at work.
She was quite skilled in the art—a pleasure to watch. She
was finishing the top part of a vase. As the wheel was spin-
ning, her fingers and thumbs were smoothing, shaping,
pulling, pushing . . . she never looked up at those who were
watching her.

While finishing the process, a part of the top of the vase
displeased her. It looked fine to me, but not to her. In the
simplest of ways, she reached over, and with a little instru-
ment she peeled off that part and remade it. Still it wasn't
the way she wanted it. Again it looked excellent to me, but it
wasn't what she liked. I was tempted to say, "That looks
fine. Leave it alone!" But I'm glad I didn't. She remade it yet
again, and it was more beautiful than ever. As she pulled
out the clay ever so slightly, what finally resulted was this
delicate flare at the top of the vase. She gave a slight nod, as
if to say, "There, that's what I wanted it to look like." Then
she left it alone. Finally, she looked at us and smiled as we
quietly applauded.

When we observed her artistry, we were impressed with
the care she had demonstrated. No detail was unimportant.
The clay had to be just right.

That's what Jeremiah witnessed as he saw the potter at
work. Then the Lord drew an analogy for His prophet.

> Then the word of the Lord came to me saying, "Can I not,
> O house of Israel, deal with you as this potter does?" declares
> the Lord. "Behold, like the clay in the potter's hand, so are
> you in My hand, O house of Israel" (vv. 5-6).

You see change written there without even finding the
word.

"You're like a lump of clay to Me, Israel. And I can shape you, hollow you out, thin your walls, and flare the top. I can make you decorative, or I can reshape you and start all over again, because change is My specialty. And you are the object of My attention and affection!"

From Jeremiah, we turn back to another prophet, Isaiah is his name.

> But now, O Lord, Thou art our Father, we are the clay, and Thou our potter (Isa.64:8).

Can you recall which gospel song came from this verse of Scripture?

> Have Thine own way, Lord!
> Have Thine own way!
> Thou art the potter, I am the clay!
> Mold me and make me after Thy will,
> While I am waiting yielded and still.[2]

Once again, it is the idea of our Lord's shaping us and changing us whichever way He pleases.

Would it help to see a living flesh-and-blood example of that? His name was Saul. He became a king. Shortly after being appointed the first king over the nation of Israel, Saul heard these words:

> Then the Spirit of the Lord will come upon you mightily, and you shall prophesy with them and be changed into another man. And it shall be when these signs come to you, do for yourself what the occasion requires; for God is with you. And you shall go down before me to Gilgal; and behold, I will come down to you to offer burnt offerings and sacrifice peace offerings. You shall wait seven days until I come to you and show you what you do.
> Then it happened when he turned his back to leave Samuel, God changed his heart; and all those signs came about on that day (1 Sam. 10:6-9).

Now I wish all changes were that rapid and that easy. Usually, changes take time and pain on our part—and much patience on God's part. But God is committed to our being changed, no matter how long or how painful the process. Never forget that! While being changed we may feel like a shapeless mass. We can't understand His reasons, like I couldn't understand the potter as she worked on her vase. But trust the Father. He's changing you. He knows what He's about.

Let's look at one more example from the Old Testament— a wonderful promise from the proverbs of Solomon. When you think about the political scene of our day, you will find great peace in this verse.

> The king's heart is like channels of water in the hand of the Lord; He turns it wherever He wishes (Prov. 21:1).

When God is ready to change a heart, it gets changed, whether it's a proud king, a stubborn husband, a strong-willed athlete, one of your own family members, or you. He turns it wherever . . . wherever He wishes. No one is an "impossible case" to God. Not even you!

The New Testament

In the New Testament we have more familiar passages of Scripture. It shouldn't take us long to survey a few of these. There is no way we can bypass Romans 8. I love this passage!

> And in the same way the Spirit also helps our weakness; for we do not know how to pray as we should, but the Spirit Himself intercedes for us with groanings too deep for words; and He who searches the hearts knows what the mind of the Spirit is, because He intercedes for the saints according to the will of God. And we know that God causes all things to work together for good to those who love God, to those who are called according to His purpose. For whom He foreknew, He also predestined to become conformed to the image of His Son, that He might be the first-born among many brethren (vv. 26-29).

God is committed to the task of conforming you and me to the image of His Son. Not physically—He's not making us look like Jesus looked physically—but inwardly: in character, in patience, in gentleness, in goodness, in grace, in truth, in discipline. He's committed to conforming our lives to the inner character of His Son.

Years ago I worked as an apprentice in a machine shop. One of the lathes I learned to operate was a tracer lathe. It had an air-controlled "finger" that traced its way along a fixed template. The template was an exact pattern of what was to be turned out on the lathe. And as this very sensitive little finger followed along the template, its every movement caused the tool that was cutting the metal to cut that exact shape. When I finished, I had a finished product from the lathe that was a precise replica of the template.

Again, that is the Father's specialty. He places His finger on the template—His Son. And He watches over His workmanship. At times the tool bites in, causing the heat to increase because of the friction. We squirm and may even try to get away. But we are His workmanship and the Father won't let us go. He holds us tightly in the lathe of His will. His goal is that we bear the image of His Son. That's the Father's task. He's committed to it. He's changing us.

Speaking of our being the Father's workmanship, look at Ephesians 2:10. Another verse brimming with encouragement!

> For we are His workmanship, created in Christ Jesus for good works, which God prepared beforehand, that we should walk in them.

Look again at those first five words: "For we are His workmanship." We're His project. He's got His eye on us. He knows what our tomorrow holds. Early every January He knows what the year will hold for us. And He is working on His project all year long. He's shaping and molding and making us like He wants us to become.

Let's glance at just one more before we look more closely at three people whose lives were changed by Jesus. Lest you think He's going to give up, lest you think He's going to back off (even though you beg Him to) this verse says He won't:

Growing Deep in the Christian Life: The Trinity

For I am confident of this very thing, that He who began a good work in you will perfect it until the day of Christ Jesus (Phil. 1:6).

What God starts, God finishes. He's never been known to walk away from an individual and say, "He's just too stubborn for Me. He is too much of a job." Kind of like some do with their teenagers. "They're just too much. I'll just leave 'em with the Lord." Well, He'll never say that. He's never met a teenager that's His match. He's never met a thirty-year-old that's His match. Any ministers reading this? He's never met a *preacher* that's His match. How about someone in their eighties or nineties? He's never met a senior citizen that's His match. God will complete what He starts—including you. It may seem unfair, it may be painful, it may involve changes that cause you to question His goodness. But He knows what is necessary.

When God wants to drill a man,
And thrill a man,
And skill a man,
When God wants to mold a man
To play the noblest part;
When He yearns with all His heart
To create so great and bold a man
That all the world shall be amazed,
Watch His methods, watch His ways!
How He ruthlessly perfects
Whom He royally elects!
How He hammers him and hurts him,
And with mighty blows converts him
Into trial shapes of clay which
Only God understands;
While his tortured heart is crying
And he lifts beseeching hands
How He bends but never breaks
When his good He undertakes;
How He uses whom He chooses,
And with every purpose fuses him;

By every act induces him
To try His splendor out—
God knows what He's about.[3]

Root Issues

1. Project yourself *back* ten years. Do your best to recall where you were living, what you were involved in, what you were concerned about, what you struggled with, where you were in your walk with Christ. Can you do it? Now, ask yourself the tough questions: How much have I *grown* during these past ten years? How is my life different? If you can see real strides in your knowledge, discernment, relationship with Christ, and in demonstrating the fruits of the Spirit (Gal. 5:22-23), take time to praise your Lord for His gracious leading and work in your heart. If you're discouraged by what you see, claim the truth of Philippians 3:12-14 and press on! He promises to be at work in our lives as we yield to Him (Phil. 2:13).

2. The Samaritan woman went to the village well at noon on one "ordinary" day, expecting to draw her usual day's ration of water. Instead, she came face to face with the living God. And her life was changed forever. Do you imagine that your tomorrow will be just like your yesterday—that nothing could lift you out of your well-worn rut? Sounds like you've stopped believing in a God with the power to bring *change*. He can make it happen! He can shatter old habits, blast apart old attitudes, wash away old resentments and hurts, push aside old fears and limitations and stereotypes. Yes, He can! Begin your tomorrow by meditating on Philippians 2:13 and Colossians 1:29. It's HIS energy that's at work in our lives, making the difference. Ask your Father to cleanse you, fill you with His Spirit, and use you in *any* way He sees fit. Then watch Him go to work!

3. Know a "doubting Thomas" who is struggling in his or her sorrow and perplexity with the reality of a loving God?

Perhaps others have already written this individual off. Don't you do it! Take time this week to make contact with your wounded friend—a call or a note or a visit. Don't judge or preach. Just assure him or her of your friendship and concern, *no matter what.* Then keep praying. The Lord has a way with tenderhearted Thomases.

Extending Your Roots

A devotional is based on a short selection of Scripture or words. Spend time praying and thinking about the passage until the Holy Spirit shows you a way to apply the truth to your life.

1. Using Jeremiah 18:1-6, write a short devotional for use in your personal quiet time with God.

Devotional Study Outline
Date:
1. Scripture/word selection:

2. Prayer/meditation:

3. Application to my life:

2. Compare your life to a lump of clay in the potter's hand. List some areas of your life that may need reshaping.

Changing Lives Is Jesus' Business

 *Taproot*

Memorizing is the retaining of knowledge of past events, ideas, or specific areas of study.

1. The selected memory verse is Philippians 1:6. Write the Scripture and reference on a small card to carry with you. Underline key words in the verse. Resource: A study Bible, Bible dictionary, Bible handbook, or Bible commentary.

Answer these questions about Philippians.
* Who wrote the letter?_____
* When was the letter written?_____
* Where was it written?_____
* What were the Philippian Christians experiencing?

* Why is this verse meaningful to you?

Review the verse every day until you can say it from memory.

2. Do you like a challenge? Try memorizing one new verse a week for one month. Suggested verses are:

1 John 1:9	1 John 5:11-12	John 14:6
Romans 5:8	Acts 16:31	1 Peter 2:24
John 3:16	Romans 8:28	Proverbs 3:4-6

17 | Three Lives Jesus Changed

I find in the Gospel by John three gripping illustrations of people who were changed. They were as different as snow-flakes, but all three were like pieces of clay on the potter's wheel. And in each slice of life that is revealed in John's Gospel, we witness a remarkable change.

There's hope here. If our Lord could change them, He can do the same today. Who were they? One, a wayward woman; another, a blind beggar; and a third, a doubting disciple. There are differences here in sex, physical ability, age, mar-ital status, and occupation. I've chosen different ones on purpose so that we'll be able to identify with at least one of the three.

A Wayward Woman: John 4

The scene occurs by a well in Samaria. The two people have never met before. One is a woman and the other is a man. The woman is never named here or elsewhere in Scrip-ture. It happens at noon. The Samaritan sun is burning down. And Jesus, hot from His journey, sits down alone by a well. His disciples have gone for food. A woman walks up to draw water. She's in for a change and doesn't know it—not yet, that is.

That's the way it happens, by the way. That's what makes life exciting. You think tomorrow is going to be your basic dull, bland tomorrow. It's not. It's very possible that a change is on the horizon.

Here's a woman who has no idea of who or what is in front

of her. As she walks up to the well she hears a Jew—a *Jew,* mind you—speaking to her, a Samaritan.

"Give Me a drink," He says.

Now you can't appreciate that, not being Jewish (and certainly not being Samaritan). You haven't seen prejudice like they knew it then. I mean, if a Jew were going to go from his homeland in Judea up north, instead of going through Samaria he went all the way around Samaria and then went further in his journey. It's sort of like going from Texas to Kansas, but choosing to travel *around* Oklahoma. Anything to keep from encountering Samaritans!

I gave that illustration some time ago. When I finished my talk I had three huge fellas corner me. All three were from Oklahoma. Almost in unison—and with a smile—they said, "We jus' want you to know we ain't got any Samaritans livin' in Oklahoma!" I've never felt more in the minority!

Remember now, His disciples had gone into the city to get something to eat, which left Jesus alone with this woman by the well.

> The Samaritan woman therefore said to Him, "How is it that You, being a Jew, ask me for a drink since I am a Samaritan woman?" (For Jews have no dealings with Samaritans.) (John 4: 9).

She was bewildered! "Not only are You speaking to a woman on the street, you're speaking to a *Samaritan* woman. And not only are You a man . . . You're a Jewish man!" Jews in Samaria stood out like a uniformed sheriff from Savannah would stand out walking through the back alleys of Harlem.

Jesus being in Samaria would be sort of like our President and his wife spending their vacation in a terrorist camp. That's how amazing, actually how ridiculous it seemed to the Samaritan woman. "What are You, a Jew, doing in *my* territory? And of all things, You're asking me for a drink. What's with You?"

Jesus answered and said to her, "If you knew the gift of God, and who it is who says to you, 'Give Me a drink,' you would have asked Him, and He would have given you living water." She said to Him, "Sir, You have nothing to draw with and the well is deep; where then do You get that living water? You are not greater than our father Jacob, are You, who gave us the well, and drank of it himself, and his son, and his cattle?" Jesus answered and said to her, "Everyone who drinks of this water shall thirst again; but whoever drinks of the water that I shall give him shall never thirst; but the water that I shall give him shall become in him a well of water springing up to eternal life." The woman said to Him, "Sir, give me this water, so I will not be thirsty, nor come all the way here to draw" (vv. 10-15).

She said, "I'll take it. Pipe it into my house. I'll take that 'living water.' I don't like walking down here and hauling it back with this jug on my head. I'd love to have you bring the water to me." She misses the point completely.

He says to her, "Go, call your husband"(v.16).

She answers, hesitatingly,

"I have no husband.". . . You have well said, 'I have no husband'; for you have had five husbands, and the one whom you now have is not your husband; this you have said truly" (vv. 17-18).

Now that was in a day when having had five husbands was scandalous— in a time when living with a man outside of wedlock was considered shameful. In one sentence, Jesus exposes the truth as He unveils her life.

I have discovered as a minister of the gospel that there are many, many people who have secrets they don't want anybody to know—even though they may do impressive things and look heroic. All of us have feet of clay.

I read some time ago about a fellow who went into a fried chicken place in Long Beach, California, and bought a couple of chicken dinners for himself and his date late one afternoon. The young woman at the counter inadvertently gave him the proceeds from the day—a whole bag of money (much of it cash) instead of fried chicken.

Three Lives Jesus Changed

After driving to their picnic site, the two sat down to open the meal and enjoy some chicken together. They discovered a whole lot more than chicken—over $800! But he was unusual. He quickly put the money back in the bag. They got back into the car and drove all the way back. Mr. Clean got out, walked in, and became an instant hero.

By then, the manager was frantic. The guy with the bag of money looked the manager in the eye and said, "I want you to know I came by to get a couple of chicken dinners and wound up with all this money. Here." Well, the manager was thrilled to death. He said, "Oh, great, let me call the newspaper. I'm gonna have your picture put in the local paper. You're one of the most honest men I've ever heard of." To which the guy quickly responded, "Oh, no, no, no, don't do that!" Then he leaned closer and whispered, "You see, the woman I'm with is not my wife. She's, uh, somebody else's wife."[1]

Interesting, isn't it? Those who often appear to be people of character are sometimes hiding a secret. Jesus has a way of penetrating the veneer. And He does that with this wayward woman by the well.

The woman said to Him, "Sir, I perceive that You are a prophet. Our fathers worshiped in this mountain, and you people say that in Jerusalem is the place where men ought to worship" (vv. 19-20).

Obviously, she's uneasy. She doesn't want to talk about husbands.

She suddenly wants to talk about religious issues. "See that mountain over there? Now our people say that's where we're to worship. You people say folks are to worship in Jerusalem. Let's talk about the mountain in Samaria or the mountain in Jerusalem. Let's discuss theology, O great prophet."

Isn't that just like us? "Let's don't talk about the husband-wife thing; let's talk about mountains." Mountains and theology make for a lot more comfortable conversations than illicit relationships, right?

Jesus said to her, "Woman, believe Me, an hour is coming when neither in this mountain, nor in Jerusalem, shall you worship the Father. You worship that which you do not know; we worship that which we know, for salvation is from the Jews. But an hour is coming, and now is, when the true worshipers shall worship the Father in spirit and truth; for such people the Father seeks to be His worshipers. God is spirit, and those who worship Him must worship in spirit and truth." The woman said to Him, "I know that Messiah is coming (He who is called Christ); when that One comes, He will declare all things to us." Jesus said to her, "I who speak to you am He" (vv. 21-26).

And at this crucial point in the dialogue, Jesus' disciples come back. This is a great moment I don't want us to overlook. It will take a little imagination. Here are twelve hungry disciples. They have hurried back, starving to death. And as they happen upon the scene they see Jesus nose to nose with a Samaritan woman! To put it mildly, the disciples were blown away. So they responded as we probably would have, given the same circumstances.

And at this point His disciples came, and they marveled that He had been speaking with a woman; yet no one said, "What do You seek?" or "Why do You speak with her?" So the woman left her waterpot, and went into the city, and said to the men, "Come, see a man who told me all the things that I have done; this is not the Christ, is it?" They went out of the city, and were coming to Him (vv. 27-30).

The disciples are still standing there, staring. Mouths open, stomachs growling. "How could He be talking to a woman, and of all things a *Samaritan* woman? Yuck!"

In the meanwhile the disciples were requesting Him, saying, "Rabbi, eat [Yeah, we got cheeseburgers, hamburgers, fries. What do you want? C'mon, Lord, let's eat."] (v. 31).
But He said to them, "I have food to eat that you do not know about" (v. 32).

This is one of the disciples' classic moments.

The disciples therefore were saying to one another, "No one brought Him anything to eat, did he?" (v. 33).

Airhead city! I'll tell you, there were moments when these fellas were really thick. "You didn't give Him a hamburger, did ya? Somebody already gave Jesus a cheeseburger?"

Jesus said to them, "My food is to do the will of Him who sent Me, and to accomplish His work (v. 34).

"C'mon, you guys! We're not talking about literal, physical food. We're not talking about cheeseburgers. We're talking about eternal things. Get your act together! Why, there are just a few months and then a harvest. I'll tell you, time is getting short."

And do you think the woman wasn't changed?

And from that city many of the Samaritans believed in Him because of the word of the woman who testified, "He told me all the things that I have done" (v. 39).

That, by the way, is one of the prime methods Jesus uses to change us. He forces us to face the truth, the whole truth, and nothing but the truth. Isn't it vulnerable to be in His presence? But isn't it *wonderful* to be honest when we are? Just to have someone with whom we can trust our deepest fears and longings! Someone before whom we can unveil the most intimate secrets of our lives!

So when the Samaritans came to Him, they were asking Him to stay with them; and He stayed there two days (v. 40).

What He did was considered scandalous in a Jewish home, but Jesus had on His heart the eternal souls of the Samaritans. There are times tradition must bow to conviction.

And many more believed because of His word; and they were saying to the woman, "It is no longer because of what you said that we believe, for we have heard for ourselves and know that this One is indeed the Savior of the world" (vv. 41-42).

She was C-H-A-N-G-E-D! What a different woman!

I want to address something you may not agree with initially, but before you throw rocks at me, just think about it. Jesus never once told her to leave that man.

Now wait a minute. Go back and check for yourself. Her living with the man wasn't Jesus' primary concern. That wasn't the major issue. He didn't rebuke her because of her immoral life. She was an *unsaved* Samaritan. Unsaved people live like that. He didn't say to her, "Clean up your act, and then you're qualified to believe." He said, "I am Messiah. And I'll tell you all the things that you've done."

In the process of coming to know Messiah it is remarkable how Messiah is able to clean up a life later on. *Then* there is power to do so—not until. Want a little tip that will help you in your witness? Don't read people a long list of rules of spirituality en route to salvation. Let the Lord do that. You present to them the Savior. You press the issue of their relationship to the Lord Jesus. Our job isn't to clean up the fish bowl, certainly not initially. It's to fish—just fish. I rather imagine that as time passed the changed woman became intensely uncomfortable with her life-style. You can't enjoy walking with a holy God and, at the same time, continue to enjoy living with a person out of wedlock. But before a person can be expected to walk, Christ must come and live within, giving the power that is needed.

A Blind Beggar

John, chapter 9, is an equally interesting story, completely different from the first one. This story does not have to do with a woman, but a man. Not a healthy, happy man, but a blind man—a blind beggar—blind from birth. But the outcome is very similar. Like that woman from Samaria, he, too, was changed.

> And as He passed by, He saw a man blind from birth. And His disciples asked Him, saying, "Rabbi, who sinned, this man or his parents, that he should be born blind?" (vv. 1-2).

Isn't it easy to become calloused when dealing with people in need? "Case 321—here's another one, Jesus." And if you

Three Lives Jesus Changed

see enough of them along the road, as you do in the Middle East, your heart can easily become indifferent to beggars. By and by, you begin to see all beggars alike. Like some see all prisoners alike, or all harlots alike, or all patients alike. Ultimately, you begin to see all humanity alike.

And so the blind beggar became a topic of theological discussion. Not only is Jesus' answer profound, the event that followed is miraculous.

> Jesus answered, "It was neither that this man sinned, nor his parents; but it was in order that the works of God might be displayed in him. We must work the works of Him who sent Me, as long as it is day; night is coming, when no man can work. While I am in the world, I am the light of the world." When He had said this, He spat on the ground, and made clay of the spittle, and applied the clay to his eyes, and said to him, "Go, wash in the pool of Siloam" (which is translated, Sent). And so he went away and washed, and came back seeing (vv. 3-7).

Now wait. You've probably read this story so many times your excitement is pretty dull. It's just another story, just another miracle.

Don't let it be! I want you to put yourself in the sandals of first-century people who have seen nothing but the same blind beggar day after miserable day, all their lives. The community knows him well. But suddenly that same man comes back from the pool, having washed the clay from his eyes, and he can see. For the first time in his entire life, he can actually see! What strikes me as remarkable are the others' reactions.

The ninth chapter of John follows the story quite closely. In verses 8 through 12 we have the neighbors' reaction; it's astounding. In verses 13 through 34, we have the Pharisees' reaction; it's unbelievable. And in verses 35 through 41 we have Jesus' response, which is so gracious, so appropriate. Let's check the neighbors' reaction first:

> The neighbors therefore, and those who previously saw him as a beggar, were saying, "Is not this the one who used to

sit and beg?" Others were saying, "This is he"; still others were saying, "No, but he is like him." He kept saying, "I am the one" (vv. 8-9).

Can you believe it? The dear guy whose entire visual world has come alive, has to verify his identity to those folks! "I am the one. I really am the same one! I can see. Look, I can see!" He can't believe that instead of celebrating with him, the neighbors are arguing over his identity.

Now, follow their thinking here:

> Therefore they were saying to him, "How then were your eyes opened?" (v. 10).

Does that seem amazing to anybody else? No one is saying, "Bring the confetti! Somebody else bring the cream cheese, the lox, and the bagels! Let's celebrate! This guy can see!" No, they're frowning, rubbing their beards, staring intently, and looking rather suspiciously as they probe, "Tell us what happened. Exactly how did this occur?"

The man responds as openly and honestly as he can.

> He answered, "The man who is called Jesus made clay, and anointed my eyes, and said to me, 'Go to Siloam, and wash'; so I went away and washed, and I received sight" (vv. 11-12).

Well, they're stumped. And in those days when you were stumped, you hauled the guy off to the religious officials. That was safe. So they brought him to the Pharisees. Now, hold on to yourself. This is where things get downright unbelievable.

> They brought to the Pharisees him who was formerly blind. Now it was a Sabbath on the day when Jesus made the clay, and opened his eyes. Again, therefore, the Pharisees also were asking him how he received his sight. And he said to them, "He applied clay to my eyes, and I washed, and I see." Therefore some of the Pharisees were saying, "This man is not from God, because He does not keep the Sabbath." But others were saying, "How can a man who is a sinner perform such signs?" And there was a division among them (vv. 13-16).

Three Lives Jesus Changed

Remember my previous chapter on Jesus' identity, where many didn't know who Jesus was? Some said He was a sinner. Some said He was a saint. Some said He was from the devil. Others said He was John the Baptizer or one of the prophets. Here is an example of that confusion. Even the Pharisees disagreed among themselves. He couldn't be from God! No way, He's a sinner. But how could a sinner do this?"

> They said therefore to the blind man again, "What do you say about Him, since He opened your eyes?" And he said, "He is a prophet." The Jews therefore did not believe it of him, that he had been blind, and had received sight, until they called the parents of the very one who had received his sight (vv. 17-18).

Here was the beggar's only visible hope—his parents. But this dear couple is so intimidated, so scared of the Pharisees, that they bow to the pressure at their own son's expense.

> [The Jews called the parents] and questioned them, saying, "Is this your son, who you say was born blind? Then how does he now see?" His parents answered then, and said, "We know that this is our son, and that he was born blind; but how he now sees, we do not know; or who opened his eyes, we do not know. Ask him; he is of age, he shall speak for himself." His parents said this because they were afraid of the Jews; for the Jews had already agreed, that if any one should confess Him to be Christ, he should be put out of the synagogue. For this reason his parents said, "He is of age; ask him" (vv. 19-23).

Astonishing! Their fear of the Pharisees is greater than their love for their own son. Frankly, that says a great deal about the intimidating power of a religious organization. The Pharisees pounce on the man:

> So a second time they called the man who had been blind, and said to him, "Give glory to God; we know that this man is a sinner." He therefore answered, "Whether He is a sinner, I do not know; one thing I do know, that, whereas I was blind, now I see." They said therefore to him, "What did He do to you? How did He open your eyes?" He answered them, "I told you already, and you did not listen; why do you want to

hear it again? You do not want to become His disciples too, do you?" (vv. 24-27).

Isn't that a great question? He's getting gutsy, isn't he? Pushing an elbow into the side of one of the hotshots, he jabs: "You're not getting a little interested, are you?"

I love that. The man has not only changed physically, he is already changing in his personality. The beggar is getting bold.

> And they reviled him, and said, "You are His disciple; but we are disciples of Moses. We know that God has spoken to Moses; but as for this man, we do not know where He is from." The man answered and said to them, "Well, here is an amazing thing, that you do not know where He is from, and yet He opened my eyes. We know that God does not hear sinners; but if anyone is God-fearing, and does His will, He hears him. Since the beginning of time it has never been heard that anyone opened the eyes of a person born blind. If this man were not from God, He could do nothing." They answered and said to him, "You were born entirely in sins, and are you teaching us?" And they put him out (vv. 28-34).

I never read this section of Scripture without realizing again just how suspicious people are about our being changed by Christ. I'll tell you, when your eyes are opened, when the blindness is removed, and especially when you begin to tell the story of your pilgrimage from blindness to faith in Christ, hang on! And don't be surprised if you encounter the most resistance from religious people. They will look at you like an alien from a galaxy far, far away. They will stare. They will really begin to wonder if you've got both oars in the water. Religious folks are uncomfortable around authentic people whose lives have been changed by the living Christ.

So the man stumbles out of their presence. Why? They put him out! And Jesus comes along and finds him. He always does.

> Jesus heard that they had put him out; and finding him, He said, "Do you believe in the Son of Man?" He answered

and said, "And who is He, Lord, that I may believe in Him?" (vv. 35-36).

You see, the man has physical sight, but not spiritual sight—not yet. He's not yet a believer. He just had his eyes opened. Now the Lord opens his heart and moves in.

Jesus said to him, "You have both seen Him, and He is the one who is talking with you." And he said, "Lord, I believe." And he worshiped Him (vv. 37-38).

Sometimes the Lord changes us physically. On other occasions, it is His plan to change a rebellious heart. Or an unforgiving spirit. Sometimes it's the inability to forgive; we're eaten up with the cancer—the internal acid of resentment and bitterness, and then the Lord graciously changes us. Occasionally the change takes place through people, sometimes alone. Occasionally the change takes place in a moment, sometimes it takes time—months, maybe years. But when it is finally complete, it sets us free. As in the case of the blind beggar, we can see. At last, we're free to see!

A Doubting Disciple

I especially like this third story. It's the briefest of the three, but perhaps the most personal for the Christian. Here is a man named Thomas who is a follower of Jesus. Before going any further, a warning is in order. We should not be too hard on him. I've spent too many hours in my ministry shooting at Thomas—and hearing others do the same. Frankly, I have matured enough over the past several years so that I see the man in a little different light having had some doubts myself, not unlike Thomas. John 20 records his response, which has been attacked for generations.

But Thomas, one of the twelve, called Didymus, was not with them when Jesus came. The other disciples therefore were saying to him, "We have seen the Lord!" But he said to them, "Unless I shall see in His hands the imprint of the nails, and put my finger into the place of the nails, and put my hand into His side, I will not believe" (vv. 24-25).

This is the same one who had earlier demonstrated a

strong faith. When Jesus talked about going to see Lazarus, Thomas had suggested, "Let us also go, that we may die with Him" (11:16). The man was committed. He was ready to go to death with his Lord. Not too many of the twelve were ready to die for Him. He's the kind of guy that when he gives himself to someone, he unloads the truck. He gives with all of his heart. He sells out wholesale—lock, stock, and barrel. "Everything I have is the Lord's." The more I think about him, the more I believe Thomas was a heart-and-soul disciple.

The problem with a man or woman like that is that when they become disillusioned, the response creates a drastic swing of the pendulum. When they back off, they fall way back. With extreme caution they start to look at things from a safe distance. "I'm not gonna get burned again. I mean, next time it's gonna take the Rock of Gibraltar before I'll give myself." Again, I suggest, that's Thomas. "I believed once. I was ready to die for Him. But everything suddenly collapsed. I saw Him go to the cross. I watched all my dreams nailed to His hands and His feet. I saw Him die. I saw them bury Him. I've seen the tomb. Looks to me like the whole shootin' match has gone up in smoke."

Then suddenly, everybody around him started talking resurrection. Some even said they had actually seen the resurrected Christ. Remember, he hadn't been in the room when Jesus showed them His hands and His side (vv. 20, 24).

While his buddies were saying, "Hey, Tom! We've seen the Lord . . . He's come back from beyond," Thomas was holding back. "Wait a minute, unless I can see what you've seen, no way am I going to believe it!" After all, they were excited because they had seen Jesus; Thomas hadn't. And I think Jesus understood the man's reluctance and reservations. If it were any other way, our Lord Jesus would have been far more severe with Thomas. Check it out for yourself. He wasn't. You'll look in vain to find a strong rebuke from Jesus. He helps people who struggle. Frankly, there are a lot of folks like Thomas. Not everybody finds it easy to believe.

> And after eight days again His disciples were inside, and Thomas with them. Jesus came, the doors having been shut, and stood in their midst, and said, "Peace be with you." Then He said to Thomas, "Reach here your finger, and see My hands; and reach here your hand, and put it into my side; and be not unbelieving, but believing" (vv. 26-27).

Jesus had not been present when Thomas had expressed his reluctance to believe, but He knows all about it. He said, in effect, "Thomas, you asked for this earlier. Here are My hands."

Thomas doesn't wrestle, doesn't argue. He doesn't stomp out of the room. He says, "My Lord and my God!" (v. 28). His doubts instantly vanish. And the disciple, like the woman at the well and the beggar on the street, is a changed man. And why not? Changing lives is Jesus' business.

Clarence Macartney writes colorful words about this scene. I have read them over and over. Take your time:

> Without any warrant for it whatsoever, Thomas had been called the Rationalist of the Apostolic Band. . . . The rationalist, the ordinary skeptic, as we think of him as and as we experience him, is not looking for signs of truth in Christianity but for signs of its falsehood. He will ferret out some little seeming discrepancy of the Biblical records and magnify it into a mountain, whereas the mighty panorama of Christian history and influence fades into nothingness. . . .
>
> Thomas, it is true, asked for signs, for particular evidence, but to liken him to the rationalist, to the skeptic, in the common use of that term is to do him a great injustice and to wrest the Scriptures. The difference between the rationalist and Thomas is this: the rationalist wants to disbelieve; Thomas wanted to believe. The rationalist, of the honest type, is occasioned by study, by examination of evidence, by the pressing bounds of the natural world, making the other world seem unreal; but the doubt of Thomas was the doubt born of sorrow.
>
> This is the deepest doubt of all, the doubt born of sorrow; that is, the doubt which rises out of the experience of our lives. The great doubts are not those that are born in Germany, in the study of the critic, in the debate of religions, nor

are they born in the laboratory, from the study of the laws of nature; they are not born of meditating over the rocks and the stars and the planets, of tracing out genealogies and chronologies; they are born in the library and in the laboratory of the soul; they are the dark interrogations cast by the experiences through which we pass in this strange adventure men call life. The doubt of a man who talks of the impossibility of a Virgin Birth is one thing; but let it not be confused with the doubt of a mother who has lost her firstborn child and wonders if God is and if her child still lives. The doubt of a man who questions the Mosaic account of the Creation of the world is one thing, but let it not be confused with the doubt of the man who sees the world in travail and sore anguish, the ceaseless invasion of hate and the eternal enmity of the evil for the good, the inhumanity of man to man, and wonders if God has forsaken His world. The doubt of Thomas was not that of a quibbler, of a cold-blooded, dilettante student; it was the doubt of a man who had lost his Lord and Master. Sorrow had filled his heart.[2]

And don't tell me you haven't had doubts like that. I can assure you, I have. And in those doubting moments when the lights are out, the valley's deep, the walls are high, thick, and cold, and tomorrow seems bleak, we also say, "He'll have to prove it to me next time." And the wonderful thing is this: He does! He comes in like a flood and shows you His hands, and He shows you His side. And He says, "Here, My child, look here, here's *proof.*"

Where Are You?

I don't know where you fit into this chapter—whether you're the wayward woman, the blind beggar, the doubting disciple—or maybe a mixture of the three. I don't need to know. I care that *you* know where you are and that you see the application. But I know it's impossible for you to be too far gone to change. You're smart enough to figure that out. You see what this chapter has been saying, don't you? The One who changes is committed to your changing as much as He was to the woman by the well, the blind beggar in the streets, the disciple who doubted; and He will not give up.

Three Lives Jesus Changed

You are like soft clay in His hands; He is going to change you. It's just a matter of time.

Won't you let Him do so with less resistance? Won't you make the trip a little bit easier? Won't you relax and let Him have His way? Isn't it about time? Yes, it is. Read again the words from that grand old hymn.

Only this time *mean* it.

Have Thine own way, Lord!
Have Thine own way!
Thou art the potter, I am the clay!
Mold me and make me After Thy will,
While I am waiting, yielded and still.

Extending Your Roots

Have you ever had doubts about who Jesus is? Most Christians do at least once. Did you know that John the Baptist doubted? Even though Jesus had changed John's life, a time came when John needed proof about Jesus' identity.

1. Complete the following interview as though you are John the Baptist. The references for your answers are Malachi 4:5-6; Matthew 3:13-17: 11:2-6; Mark 1:2-11: 6:17-20; Luke 3:21-22: 7:18-23; and John 1:37.

Scene: A Jerusalem prison

Interviewer: John, let me introduce myself. I am a person whose life has been changed by Jesus Christ and I am interested in your life and how Jesus changed you. Would you mind answering a few questions?

John the Baptist: I'll be happy to.

I: When did you first meet Jesus?

JB:

I: Some people say you fulfilled an Old Testament prophecy. Is this true?

Growing Deep in the Christian Life: The Trinity

JB:

I: What was your primary message?
JB:

I: Did some of your disciples follow Jesus?
JB:

I: The Scriptures indicate that you had some doubts about Jesus.
JB:

I: How did you handle your doubts?
JB:

(Interview stops.)
   2. Name some ways of handling doubts.

What can you do to overcome doubts about Jesus?

Three Lives Jesus Changed

Taproot

Doubting moments occur in almost everyone's mind. However, Jesus can change doubts to deliverance.

1. Read about some Bible doubters and how God accomplished His will through their lives.

Scripture	*Doubter*	*Doubt*
Genesis 17:17		
Exodus 3:10-15		
Judges 6:14-23		
John 20:24-25		

2. Are you struggling with any doubts?
List them in the space below.

3. Ask Jesus to change your doubts to complete belief and understanding.

Part III

The
Holy
Spirit

18 | The Spirit Who Is Not a Ghost

I did an "unearthly" thing last week. In fact, I did it twice.

Thinking back over my lifetime (which is now more than five decades), I have done many adventurous things. I've even done a few crazy things; some I think would qualify as mischievous, risky, and on a few occasions, dangerous. To retain the little bit of respect I have built with my readers over the years, I am not going to reveal all of those things that I have done. But I have to tell you about this unearthly thing I did twice this past week.

By the way, I checked Webster's for *unearthly* to make sure it's the word I want. It means "nonterrestrial, not mundane . . . weird." So *unearthly* is the right word. Being an earthling, I found it to be wonderful—downright exciting.

I defied gravity.

Now I have to confess I didn't do it on my own—earthlings can't do that, you see. I needed help from a power outside myself, and that posed a bit of a problem because that power happens to be invisible. And that's where things got a little "eerie." How did I know it was invisible? I looked. As a matter of fact, I stared. I leaned over the fella sitting next to the window, and I watched the wings as we roared down the runway with the jets full throttle. I kept looking to see if I could see the power that would make my unearthly experience happen.

Finally, the guy sitting next to the window said to me, "Are you all right?"

"Yes," I said, as I kept staring at the wing, "I'm just

145

checking." (I like saying things like that when you're taking off in airplanes.) And before long he was looking back and checking with me!

"What are we checking for?" he asked, as he strained his neck.

"Well," I replied, "we're looking for the stuff that holds us up." That led into a very interesting conversation, I might add.

You say, "Aw, Chuck, gimme a break. Here I was thinking you did something spooky, like *really* weird, but you just flew." You're right, that's exactly what I did. But you have to admit, even though it's now a common thing, it is still amazing. That invisible force held our plane 30,000 feet above sea level for well over two hours both going and coming. And not one of us inside the plane ever saw what did it. To borrow a line from a couple of now-famous movies, "the force was with us." Invisible, yet present.

Air is a force with incredible strength. It can snap a tree in two or demolish a landscape. Given enough velocity, air becomes a devastating wind. Energized by a hurricane or tornado, it can clear out an entire mobile home park in seconds. The power in that invisible stuff! If you contain it in a network of hoses and valves and put it under enough pressure, it can bring a massive commercial bus or truck-trailer rig to a screeching halt. It'll even stop a locomotive pulling over a hundred cars. It will break thick concrete on a driveway or a freeway if it's pushed through the right tools. It will loosen or tighten the lug nuts on your car's wheels if funneled into the right mechanism. In fact, it can lift massive amounts of weight.

The manager of a granite quarry in North Carolina once said,

> We supplied the granite for the municipal building in New York City. We can lift an acre of solid granite ten feet thick to almost any height we desire for the purpose of moving it .... We can do it as easily as I can lift a piece of paper.[1]

How? Air. That's all, just air.

You can't feel it. You can't see it or smell it (unless you live around Los Angeles!). You can't, except in most technical ways, measure it or weigh it. But it keeps you alive every minute. If I took air away from you who are now reading this book for five minutes, you would become brain damaged. We cannot live without it. Yet when we fly, apply our brakes, or watch a mechanic work on our car, we think nothing of it. Amazing stuff, air.

Never think that because something is invisible it is therefore unimportant or weak. You may be surprised to know that the Bible talks a lot about air. The Old Testament calls it *ruach*. The New Testament calls it *pneuma*. We get the word *pneumatic* from the New Testament Greek word. The English Bible, however, doesn't translate either one as *air*. Usually, it's *breath*. "God breathed into man the breath of life." Or it's called *wind*. "Like a mighty wind." Or it is translated *spirit*—as in the "spirit of man" or "the Holy Spirit."

A number of synonyms are used for Spirit—words like *helper, advocate, comforter, convicter, restrainer, exhorter,* and *reprover*. He is portrayed by symbols, too, such as a dove, fire, wind, even water. In John 7 we read of this power being called "living water."

Jesus is speaking:

> If any man is thirsty, let him come to Me and drink. He who believes in Me, as the Scripture said, "From his innermost being shall flow rivers of living water" (vv. 37-38).

And in case you wonder what He had reference to, the next verse explains:

> But this He spoke of the Spirit (v. 39).

He referred to the Spirit of God, the third member of the Trinity.

Let me paraphrase verse 38: "From the believer's inner life there will be a reservoir of enormous, immeasurable power. It will gush forth. It will pour out like a torrential river that causes rapids, waterfalls, and endless movement to the ocean." That's the idea. It's not a picture of some blasé, passive force. The Spirit of God is the dynamic of life. Like air, the Spirit may be invisible—but let us never be misled by equating invisible with impotent. This Spirit is vital to life.

We are so impressed with what we can touch and weigh and see that when it comes to something that is invisible, we pass it off. We get so used to that power that we tend to think nothing more of the force than a Monday-morning flight. Christians all around the world need the reminder that the most powerful force in life is something we can't even see . . . so powerful we are secured eternally until Christ comes, turning our destiny into reality, ushering us into eternity. I call that powerful. And until that time, He is ready to work within us and move among us in revolutionary ways, transforming our lives. No, never think that something is insignificant because it's invisible.

Root Issues

1. Is the Holy Spirit "a real and relevant force" in your life? This will take a little thought. Open your notebook and take a few minutes to jot down the five biggest challenges facing you in your life these days. Name them and number them. Now, can you feel the weight of those daily struggles bite into your shoulders—that old tightness in the pit of your stomach? Let the heaviness of your list pull you down to your knees. Ask your Father to show you what it means to have the Spirit of God resident *within* you. Ask Him to shoulder the weight of these constant struggles (1 Pet. 5:7). Consciously yield your challenges to the Helper's control—to His invisible yet limitless power (Eph. 3:16). Don't get up from your knees until your shoulders—and your heart—feel lighter.

2. When the words of Jesus at the last supper finally began to sink in, the disciples were seized with panic. They

could scarcely hear the vital information the Lord wanted to communicate to them. "I have so much to tell you," He said to them, "but I know you can't handle it right now" (see John 16:6,12). It would be later, when the hearts were quieter, that the Spirit would guide them into the truth (v. 13).

Isn't that just like us? The Spirit's still, small voice is so easily drowned out by those feelings of fear, worry, dread, or panic that we experience when life's circumstances press in on us. Yet it is precisely in those moments that He has much to share with us! The next time you find pressure mounting in your life, try this: Find a restful setting where you can be alone for thirty minutes to an hour. Find a quiet booth in a coffee shop, go for an evening walk, find a room in a church, just get away from the noise and hassle for a while. Ask the Spirit of God to quiet your heart and speak to you while you focus on your Lord and His Word. Don't miss the opportunity to hear His voice and benefit from His counsel in the midst of your struggle and pain. He is ready to help!

3. Carefully consider the fourfold prayer suggested in chapter 21—MELT me, MOLD me, FILL me, USE me. On a fresh page in your notebook jot down some *specific* ideas about what each one of these aspects of the Spirit's work could imply in your life.

Extending Your Roots

1. Replay in your mind the many ways the word *power* is used in the Bible or our favorite hymns. For a starter, think about the hymn: "There Is *Power* in the Blood."

Now jot down some references to *power*.

2. How many of these phrases or titles refer to the Holy Spirit?

3. Suppose a person asks, "What do *you* know about the Holy Spirit?" How would you reply?

4. What do the words words *air, breath, wind, spirit* have in common?

5. Complete the acrostic with words or phrases that describe the Holy Spirit.

H	S
O	P
L	I
Y	R
	I
	T

Taproot

1. Joel 2:28-32 contains a prophecy. Read several commentaries for an in-depth look at what Joel was saying. How does this prophecy clarify the title of this chapter?

19 Some Things the Holy Spirit Is Not

There are some things the Spirit of God is not. Let me point out three or four erroneous ideas that many people have about the Holy Spirit. In fact, when people return to their roots and attempt to explain their beliefs, they are often most confused about the doctrine of the Holy Spirit. I have often heard Him called an "it" . . . so let's start there.

The Spirit Is Not an "It," but a Distinct Personality

The Holy Spirit is a distinct person. He is a "Him," a "He." Jesus once said:

> If you ask Me anything in My name, I will do it. If you love Me, you will keep My commandments. And I will ask the Father, and He will give you another Helper, that *He* may be with you forever; that is the Spirit of truth, whom the world cannot receive, because it does not behold *Him* or know *Him*, but you know *Him* because *He* abides with you, and will be in you (John 14:14-17, emphasis added).

What a helpful revelation! While Jesus was on the earth, the Spirit of God was *with* the people of God. But when Jesus left the earth and sent another Helper ("another of the same kind," interestingly), like Himself, the Helper came and became a part of their lives deep within. No longer near them, but *in* them. That's a mind-staggering truth. And notice He is called "He" or "Him"—never "It." Nowhere in any reliable version of Scripture is the Spirit of God referred to as "It."

The Spirit Is Not Passive, but Active and Involved

> But I tell you the truth, it is to your advantage that I go away; for if I do not go away, the Helper shall not come to you; but if I go, I will send Him to you (John 16:7).

What will He do? Lie around, take it easy, relax, casually kick back within us? No. Read very carefully what Jesus taught:

> And He, when He comes, will convict the world concerning sin, and righteousness, and judgment. . . . But when He, the Spirit of truth, comes, He will guide you into all the truth; for He will not speak on His own initiative, but whatever He hears, He will speak; and He will disclose to you what is to come. He shall glorify Me; for He shall take of Mine, and shall disclose it to you (vv. 8, 13-14).

Oftentimes we can sense that He is present. On some occasions His presence is so real, so obvious—it's almost as though we can touch Him. When He moves among a body of people, He mobilizes and empowers them. They become sensitive, motivated, spiritually alive. They are cleansed. They are purged, enthusiastic, actively excited about the right things.

Who hasn't been in meetings where His presence made the place electric? But when He is absent, it is dreadfully dead, desperately, horribly lifeless. I have witnessed both. The contrast is undeniable.

Never doubt that the Spirit of God is incessantly on the move. As with air, we cannot see Him; nevertheless, He is hard at work convicting, guiding, instructing, disclosing, and glorifying. Just a few of His activities! He's involved. He's active. We'll return to these thoughts in a moment.

The Holy Spirit Is Not Imaginary, but Real and Relevant

Let me remind you that just because you cannot see the Holy Spirit, do not assume He is not there or is not real. Just before Jesus' ascension into heaven, He met with a group of His followers. They had questions. He had answers. He also had some crucial news regarding the Spirit who would soon come to take His place.

> And so when they had come together, they were asking Him, saying, "Lord, is it at this time You are restoring the kingdom to Israel?" He said to them, "It is not for you to know times or epochs which the Father has fixed by His own authority; but you shall receive power when the Holy Spirit has come upon you; and you shall be My witnesses both in Jerusalem, and in all Judea and Samaria, and even to the remotest part of the earth" (Acts 1:6-8).

Familiar words to many Christians, packed with significance. Note especially that the Spirit is no imaginary, vague hope; that is a promise from our Savior. It is as if He were saying, "You will have His presence, and wherever you go He will be in you. He will empower you. He will be your 'dynamic' . . . a real and relevant force in My plan for your future."

The Holy Spirit Is Not a Substitute for God, but He Is Deity

This will heighten your respect for the Holy Spirit's work, if nothing else will. Christians have been known to fight for the deity of Christ . . . and we certainly should. But what about the Deity of the Spirit? Tucked away in the Book of Acts is a seldom-mentioned story about a couple who paid the ultimate price for their hypocrisy. Woven into their brief biography is a statement of the Spirit's Deity.

> But a certain man named Ananias, with his wife Sapphira, sold a piece of property, and kept back some of the price for himself, with his wife's full knowledge, and bringing a portion of it, he laid it at the apostles' feet. But Peter said, "Ananias, why has Satan filled your heart *to lie to the Holy Spirit* and to keep back some of the price of the land? While it remained unsold, did it not remain your own? And after it was sold, was it not under your control? Why is it that you have

conceived this deed in your heart? *You have not lied to men, but to God"* (5:1-4, emphasis added).

Connect those two parts I have underscored. When they lied "to the Holy Spirit" (v. 3), they "lied, . . . to God" (v. 4).

Before going any further into this doctrinal treasure house, let me ask you to imagine what it means to have the presence of the living God within you.

Pause and ponder this, my Christian friend: The third member of the Godhead, the invisible, yet all-powerful representation of Deity, is actually living inside your being. His limitless capabilities are resident within you, since He indwells you.

You think you can't handle what life throws at you?

You think you can't stand firm or, when necessary, stand alone in your life?

You think you can't handle the lure of life's temptations? Well, you certainly could not if you were all alone. You—*alone*—can't do that any more than I can fly alone. But with the right kind of power put into operation, the very power and presence of God, you can handle it. You can do it. As a matter of fact, all the pressure will be shifted and the weight transferred from you to Him. It's a radically different way to live. And because He is God He can handle it.

I'm starting to sound a little authoritative about this awesome truth. The fact of the matter is that we know very little about how He does it—only that He is able to do it.

Reminds me of the teacher standing before a group of fifth graders. He looked over his class with a wry smile and asked, "Does anybody here understand how electricity works?" And Jimmy, one overanxious little boy sitting toward the front of the class, lifted his hand high in the air and said, "Yes, I understand electricity." A bit surprised, his teacher looked at him and said, "All right, Jimmy, would you explain electricity to the class." Jimmy suddenly put his hands over his face and said, "Oh . . . last night I knew, but this morning I've forgotten." The teacher gave this tongue-in-cheek response, "Now this is a tragedy. The only person in all of history who ever understood electricity, and this morning he forgot it!"

I confess, I'm starting to feel a little like Jimmy. The deeper we get into this subject, the more there is to discover, the more profound the Spirit is! I, therefore, must come to grips with what I *can* understand God's Book to be saying about the Holy Spirit. And I must leave the rest with Him. Like electricity, I need Him, though I cannot fully explain how He works. He is extremely useful in my life—essential, in fact—yet my ability to explain each facet of His ministry is quite limited. I need Him and I rely on Him . . . but I don't pretend to know all about Him. Once I've plugged into the socket, I've about run out of knowledge. But what I don't understand, I can still enjoy!

Don't let it trouble you if you struggle with trying to define and divide meanings of words and ideas and thoughts about the Holy Spirit. Some of these things are infinite and unfathomable.

He exists in an invisible realm. He is a power and a force you will never see, though you are convinced of the force Himself. You will only see His working—the results of His enabling, His filling, His guiding. But when He, the Spirit of God, is in control, it is nothing short of awesome. And as I said earlier, when He is absent, it is dreadful. Believe me, nothing is worse than preaching a sermon without the Spirit's help. Well, maybe one thing is worse—listening to that sermon! It is the longest period of time you can endure. As a friend of mine once said, "Without the Spirit's blessing, everything is just toothpaste."

 *Extending Your Roots*

A Doctrinal Study

"Doctrine" means something that is taught. This activity is designed to affirm what the Bible says about the Holy Spirit.

Growing Deep in the Christian Life: The Trinity

Match the statements and the Scripture references to check your understanding of the doctrine of the Holy Spirit.

1. The Holy Spirit is the Spirit of God.
2. He inspired the Scriptures.
3. He enables people to understand truth.
4. He exalts Christ.
5. He convicts of sin, righteousness, and judgment.
6. He calls people to the Savior and effects regeneration.
7. He cultivates Christian character, comforts believers, and bestows the spiritual gifts by which they serve God through His church.
8. He seals the believer unto the day of final redemption.
9. His presence in the Christian is the assurance of God to bring the believer into the fullness of the stature of Christ.
10. He enlightens and empowers the believer and the church in worship, evangelism, and service.

_____ Genesis 1:2	_____ Acts 7:55
_____ Judges 14:6	_____ Acts 8:17, 39
_____ Job 26:13	_____ Acts 10:44
_____ Psalm 51:11	_____ Acts 13:2
_____ Psalm 139:7*ff.*	_____ Acts 15:28
_____ Isaiah 61:1-3	_____ Acts 16:6
_____ Joel 2:28-32	_____ Acts 19:1-6
_____ Matthew:18	_____ Rom. 8:9-11, 14-16, 26-27
_____ Matthew 3:16	_____ 1 Corinthians 2:10-14
_____ Matthew 4:1	_____ 1 Corinthians 3:16
_____ Matthew 12:28-32	_____ 1 Corinthians 12:3-11
_____ Matthew 28:19	_____ Galatians 4:6
_____ Mark 1:10, 12	_____ Ephesians 1:13-14
_____ Luke 1:35	_____ Ephesians 4:30
_____ Luke 4:1, 18-19	_____ Ephesians 5:18
_____ Luke 11:13	_____ 1 Thessalonians 5:19
_____ Luke 12:12	_____ 1 Timothy 3:16
_____ Luke 24:49	_____ 1 Timothy 4:1
_____ John 4:24	_____ 2 Timothy 1:14
_____ John 14:16-17, 26	_____ 2 Timothy 3:16
_____ John 15:26	_____ Hebrews 9:8,14

_____ John 16:7-14   _____ 2 Peter 1:21

_____ Acts 1:8   _____ 1 John 4:13

_____ Acts 2:1-4, 38   _____ 1 John 5:6-7

_____ Acts 4:30   _____ Revelation 1:10

_____ Acts 5:3   _____ Revelation 22:17

_____ Acts 6:3

 *Taproot*

1. Choose one of the ten statements about the Holy Spirit and write an explanation based on the Scriptures that relate to the statement.

2. How can you make your new understanding of the Holy Spirit more real in your life?

20 Some Reasons the Holy Spirit Is Here

Jesus promised the Holy Spirit would come. But why? What, precisely, can we expect from Him? For some answers, let's return to John 16.

Allow me a few moments to explain the background of the words John records here. It may help you understand why the disciples seemed so dull and unable to grasp what the Lord was saying.

First of all, the hour was late—around midnight. Jesus and His disciples were in a second-story flat in Jerusalem. There were eleven men with Him. One had been dismissed—the unfaithful Judas. In this upper room the men were reclining around a table, and there was small talk. The focus of attention finally turned to the Lord Himself. In quiet tones, He began to communicate the vital truths they were to live by after His death. When they realized how *serious* He was, they were seized with panic. Why?

Keep in mind that for over three years they'd been following the man they expected to be the ruler of the world. That meant they would be charter-member officials in the kingdom. Don't think they hadn't thought of that! And He would establish Himself as King of kings and Lord of lords. He would overthrow Rome. He would move the hypocrites in the religious world out of power as He established a new rulership marked by integrity, peace, authenticity, and righteousness. That was their dream, their hope. But now, out of the clear blue, He tells them He's going to *die*. In a matter of hours He would be taken under arrest and by midmorning the next day He would be nailed to a cross. By midafternoon his body would slump in death. Before dark they will have taken His body down, wrapped Him as a mummy, put Him in a tomb, and sealed it.

He—their Teacher—would be gone.

Of course they were confused! The talk of death can't help but bring panic, cause confusion, and, in addition, create an inability to grasp a set of facts.

Before you're too harsh on them, imagine the charged emotions. Their heads must have been swimming. I can assure you it isn't hard for me to imagine. Right after World War II my father had a physical breakdown—maybe some would say an emotional breakdown. Perhaps it was both. Whichever, I shall never forget the dreadful feeling when, as the youngest in a family of three children, I was called into his bedroom. I can still feel his hand sort of work its way from my elbow up to my shoulder. I still remember how he held me close as he trembled (though he wasn't an old man), exhausted from the rigors of endless work—sixteen- to eighteen-hour days, six to seven days a week, for four or five years of his life. I knew I might never see my dad again on this earth. At least, I thought I wouldn't. He gave me some information about life. He talked to me quietly and deliberately about the character he wanted me to model as I grew up without him. He told me to take care of my mother and to cooperate with my brother and sister. I shall never forget choking back the tears.

I am pleased to say he lived on. In fact, he lived many years beyond that. But at that time, if my life depended on it, when I walked out of the room that dark night, I couldn't tell you precisely what he had said or what his words meant. I had only one thing on my mind: "My daddy is gonna die!" That stabbing realization eclipsed everything else he said. It may have been important, but I missed it. I can still recall a few words he used, but that's about it. Death talk is like that.

That's what happened to those disciples. They're listening to the Messiah say: "I'm going to die, but don't worry . . . I won't leave you as orphans. I'm going to send another Helper."

They thought, *Another Helper? We want You. We don't want someone else.*

He added, "He will be even more helpful to you than I am, because He will be everywhere at once. And He'll be within you, not just by your side."

They resisted within—"We don't want that." You know that kind of feeling, and that's what blocked their ability to grasp words that seem so clear to us today . . . the words John records in chapter 16.

Now centuries have passed. And we've been able to work through these verses with the help of history to guide our thoughts. In fact, we've got the verbs, prepositions, nouns, subjects, and predicates down pat. But those people merely heard these words. No one had written anything down at the time. That's why they responded like they did. "Sorrow filled their hearts," according to verse 6. The word is *grief*. They were grieving over the imminent loss of their Savior, their Lord, their Friend. Even later when He was raised from the dead, they struggled to believe it. Once they convinced themselves of His death, the resurrection was almost impossible to accept. Remember Thomas in the previous chapter? He demanded to see the prints in Jesus' hands, in His feet, and in His side—the literal scars of death. These men had been convinced that He would live on and on, but now He says:

> But because I have said these things to you, sorrow has filled your heart. But I tell you the truth, it is to your advantage that I go away; for if I do not go away, the Helper shall not come to you; but if I go, I will send Him to you (vv. 6-7).

Why would it be more advantageous to them that the Helper come? Well, when the Lord Jesus was on earth, He was shackled by the body that had been formed in Mary's womb, which became visible at Bethlehem. He could be only one place at a time. But when the Spirit came, He would be everywhere at once. And within each one of them—and us! Isn't that remarkable? No matter where you are, He is there. And He is ready to help. You never wake Him up. He who watches over you is never interrupted when you call for assistance. Morning, noon, or the middle of the night, He's available. He'll give power. He'll guide. He'll comfort, sustain, instruct, protect, enable.

Furthermore, by having Him invisible, their faith would be strengthened. It doesn't take any faith to fly if King Kong lifts the plane up and carries it from Los Angeles and then sets it down on the runway in Dallas. That's not faith. You just wait until Kong puts you back down again. And you get out of the plane. But when you have to rely on something invisible, it gets a little shaky at times. That's why Jesus' words to Thomas apply to all generations.

> Jesus said to him, "Because you have seen Me, have you believed? Blessed are they who did not see, and yet believed" (20:29).

Some Work the Holy Spirit Accomplishes

> And He, when He comes, will convict the world concerning sin, and righteousness, and judgment; concerning sin, because they do not believe in Me; and concerning righteousness, because I go to the Father, and you no longer behold Me; and concerning judgment, because the ruler of this world has been judged. I have many more things to say to you, but you cannot bear them now (16:8-12).

In this section Jesus talks first about the Holy Spirit's ministry among non-Christians. Later He talks about His ministry among Christians.

Among Non-Christians

You may be surprised to know that the Spirit is involved in the unsaved world. He works among the unsaved at all times. As a matter of fact, in one of the letters to the Thessalonians, we read that He is actively involved restraining sin (2 Thess. 2:7). Do you have any idea how much evil would be on this earth if the Spirit of God were suddenly removed? His omnipresence is like a worldwide envelope of righteousness, a bubble of invisible restraint. He holds a great deal of evil in check. But when He is is removed, literally all hell will break loose on this globe! Thankfully, He currently restrains sin.

Earlier we read that the same Holy Spirit "convicts the world concerning sin, righteousness, and judgment." I am comforted when I read that. It frees me from the need to moralize when I'm in a group of unsaved people. I don't have to try to convince lost people about how unrighteous they are. They already know they're unrighteous. How? The Spirit is already convincing them! I don't have to fly a big flag over my home that reads, "We're pure and holy— you're dirty and nasty." My ministry is not to convince someone else that they're really bad people. That's the Spirit's ministry. "He convicts the world of sin, because they do not believe on Me." His convicting work is much more effective than mine ever could be.

The late Merrill Tenney offers a timely word regarding the meaning of *convict*:

> "Convict" means to refute an adversary completely, to prove guilt so as to bring an acknowledgment of the truth of the charge. It implies a successful action against an opponent that results in establishing his guilt.[1]

The word is a legal term that means to pronounce a judicial verdict by which the guilt of the culprit at the bar of justice is defined and fixed! The Spirit does not merely *ACCUSE*
men of sin, He brings them an inescapable sense of guilt so that they realize their shame and helplessness before God. The Holy Spirit performs an open-and-shut case of convincing.

This reminds me of that unforgettable day the prophet Nathan stood before David who had committed adultery with Bathsheba. The king was cornered when she became pregnant, so he manipulated the death of Uriah, her husband. And then he lied about it to his flock of people, the nation. He lived that lie for a year, until Nathan came and stood before him. And after a brief parable regarding taking someone else's little ewe lamb, he stared directly at David and said, "You are the man!" And David, without hesitation, responded, "I have sinned." In other words, "Guilty as charged!" That's the way it is when the Spirit works.

Many without Christ struggle with their guilt and unbelief. You'd better believe it! They try every way in the world to run away from it—through a bottle, through drugs, through travel, through activity, through education, through philosophy of some kind or another, or through some other means of escape. It's the inescapable guilt that haunts them.

The Spirit not only convicts the world of sin but also of righteousness. He is like the prosecuting attorney saying, "These are the facts. Here is the evidence. All these things demonstrate guilt." And they are shut up without excuse in light of facts and evidence. There is simply no way the lost can measure up to God's righteous demands. They may try, but the Spirit of God will convince them of their need.

Catalina Island lies twenty-six miles from our California shoreline. I could probably locate several folks down at Huntington Beach who can jump off the pier out into the ocean fifteen or so feet. A few could jump twenty feet. We may find a triathlete or a decathelete who can jump twenty-five feet. But we'll never find anyone who can jump all the way to Catalina. No one on earth can do that. If you want to get to Catalina, you have to take a boat.

The Spirit of God makes it clear that all have sinned and fall short of perfection. Every person who comes into the family of God has been worked on ahead of time by the Spirit. And His irresistible ministry has been, "You are guilty. You are lost. You are a sinner. You are separated from God. You are spiritually depraved. You are distant from God, without hope, lacking in righteousness. You must have Christ in order to measure up to the standard of perfection God requires."

And judgment? Jesus also taught that the Spirit would convince the world of judgment.

He, when He comes, will convict the world concerning judgment . . . because the ruler of this world has been judged (vv. 8, 11).

When human sin is confronted by the righteousness of Christ, inevitable judgment is evident. And the reason it's so significant is because the ruler of this world (Satan himself) stands judged. That means that Satan was judged at the cross. And every moment that Satan exists since the cross, he stands judged. Each tick of the clock moves him closer to his doom. He's a defeated foe.

That reminds me of what happened when I taught my two boys to play chess. Bad decision on my part. Man, did they learn how to play chess! Both of them can beat me virtually every time we play. Now they *love* playing chess with me. I work hard at it—and sometimes take a long time to make a move. I'll really think it through. They go get a hamburger, eat it, come back, and about then I'll move. And what I hate is that when I finally make that move, they snicker under their breath . . . hee, hee, hee . . . I hate that laugh!

Then they'll poke some fun by asking things like, "Before you take your hands off, Dad, you wanna take that move back?"

"No!" I respond.

"OK, then watch—(bomp . . . bomp . . . bomp . . . bomp) checkmate!"

That's the way it is with the devil. Every move Satan makes is simply one move closer to the end of the game. The prince of the world stands judged.

The point is clear: If that's true of the prince of the world, it's certainly true of the lost person. When human sin is confronted by Christ's righteousness, condemnation is self-evident. Every day the unsaved person lives is one day closer to judgment. The Spirit continues to convince the lost of inevitable judgment.

One of the reasons I'm hammering away on this is because I want to take the neurotic stress out of all who evangelize. Not the zeal or the passion, but the panic. Our responsibility is to communicate the Lord Jesus, to present the righteousness of God, to tell everybody we meet as often as we can that the Lord Jesus died for them, rose from the dead for them, offering hope beyond the grave, that there is forgiveness and cleansing, a relationship with God through faith in His Son, if they will only believe. It's not our job to convince them thatthey're lost. That's the Spirit's job! We're to tell them about the bridge of hope in Jesus Christ, inviting them to "Get on it. Get on that bridge."

Among Christians

The Spirit of truth works in believers' lives as well.

> But when He, the Spirit of truth, comes, He will guide you into all the truth; for He will not speak on His own initiative, but whatever He hears, He will speak; and He will disclose to you what is to come. He shall glorify Me; for He shall take of Mine, and shall disclose it to you. All things that the Father has are Mine; therefore I said, that He takes of Mine, and will disclose it to you (vv. 13-15).

The Holy Spirit not only takes the Scriptures and makes them clear (that's the ministry of illumination which I mentioned in ch. 3), but He takes circumstances in which we find ourselves and he gives us insight into them. He takes pressure and predicaments, then uses them to mature us. He guides us into all realms of the truth. He matures us. He nurtures us. He comforts us when we are fractured by fear. He tells us there's hope when we can't see the end of the tunnel. He gives us reasons to go on, though we get up in years and it looks like death is near. All of that is included in the thought, "He guides [us] into all the truth."

The beautiful part of all this is that He doesn't speak on His own initiative. He's not on a lark, just telling us what we would like to hear. He's taking truth from "the things of Christ," and He discloses them to us. In fact, Jesus promises "He shall glorify Me."

Growing Deep in the Christian Life: The Trinity

Let me pass along something I hope you *never* forget. If you get involved in a ministry that glorifies itself, instead of Christ, the Spirit of God is not in that ministry. If you follow a leader that is getting the glory for that ministry, instead of Christ, the Spirit of God isn't empowering His leadership. If you're a part of a Christian school or a mission organization or a Christian camping ministry in which someone other than Christ is being glorified, it is not being empowered by the Spirit of God. Mark it down: THE SPIRIT GLORIFIES CHRIST. I'll go one step further; if the Holy Spirit Himself is being emphasized and magnified, He isn't in it! *Christ* is the One who is glorified when the Spirit is at work. He does His work behind the scenes, never in the limelight. I admire that the most about His work.

We Christians love to sing a chorus:

Spirit of the living God,
fall fresh on me;
Spirit of the living God,
Fall fresh on me,
Break me, melt me, mold me,
fill me.
Spirit of the living God,
Fall fresh on me.[2]

When He does these things, when He melts us and molds us, fills us and uses us, Christ alone is exalted.

Extending Your Roots

Because I have said these things, you are filled with grief. But I tell you the truth: It is for your good that I am going away. Unless I go away, the Counselor will not come to you; but if I go, I will send him to you (John 16:6-7, NIV).

1. To be sure you are familiar with the names given to the Holy Spirit in the Bible, check these verses. Write the name beside each reference.

John 16:13 _____

Romans 1:4 _____

Romans 8:2 _____

1 Corinthians 3:16 _____

2 Corinthians 4:13 _____

2 Timothy 1:7 _____

Hebrews 10:29 _____

2. The Holy Spirit helps Christians worship. Read the following verses and write down how the Spirit accomplishes His work for us.

Romans 8:26 _____

John 14:26 _____

Romans 5:5 _____

Taproot

1. Think for a minute about a Sunday morning worship service. Describe a service where the moving of the Holy Spirit is absent.

Describe a service where the moving of the Holy Spirit is present.

2. Suggest ways to ensure the Holy Spirit has freedom to do His work in your worship services.

21 | Some Ways the Holy Spirit Is Felt

You may have noticed how I've stayed away from "techniques" in our study of the Holy Spirit. I've purposely not given you five ways to be filled with the Spirit, six steps to the Spirit-filled life, nine guarantees that the Spirit is empowering you, or how to be "almost perfect" in three easy steps. But I would like to apply these truths in the area of the Spirit's *melting, molding, filling,* and *using* us. I'd like to go back to some things I said in chapter 20 and share with you my closing thoughts. Four come to my mind.

Since He Is a Person, We Feel Him as He Heals Relationships

When He does that He *melts* us. I realize that you may not have entered into the work of the Spirit in this realm. Perhaps you have big thick walls around your life, barriers of resistance, heavy fortifications that keep you distant from people. To break through those walls, a melting process is needed. Believe me, He can do that, because He wants to heal strained relationships. Maybe with your child who is now grown. Maybe with your parent. Maybe with a person who was once a very close, trusted friend. Somehow there has to be the melting work of the Spirit before such healing can happen. Ask the Spirit of God to begin melting you.

Since He Is Active and Involved, We Feel Him Comforting Us in Our Sorrows and Guiding Us in Our Pursuits

When He does that, He *molds* us. By the way, these go in order: first there's melting (as relationships are healed), and

168

not until then can there be molding. It's nothing short of amazing how such healing clears our sights, freeing us to pursue new directions. The Spirit of God's presence is there to mold us and reshape us. By the way, it can get pretty painful. At times, you are convinced that you simply cannot go on. Yet the Spirit who shapes us is also "the Comforter." He will be with you. Ask the Spirit of God to mold you.

Since He Is Real and Relevant, We Feel Him Giving Us Power and Perseverance

When He does that, He *fills* us. I often begin my day by saying something like, "Lord God, I don't know what my day holds. I don't know what's in it for You and me, but I'm Yours. I want You to guide me one step at a time. And I want Your power to mark my steps. Stop me if I'm moving in a wrong direction. Push me if I'm sluggish. Get me going again if I'm hesitant. Shake me back to my senses if I get out of line, but don't let me go my own way. Fill me today with Your peace and Your power." Because the Spirit is not imaginary, because He's real and relevant, it is remarkable how He turns that day into something else—often a marvelous series of events. Ask the Spirit of God to fill you.

Since He Is God, We Feel Him as He Controls Our Circumstances and Transforms Our Lives

When He does that, He *uses* us.

- He melts us in relationships.
- He molds us in the pursuit and the direction of His will.
- He fills us with power and perseverance to stay at it.
- He uses us as He controls our circumstances and transforms our lives.

When those things happen we become convinced we're not excess baggage. We're not models of mediocrity. We have purpose and meaning and definition—many reasons to press on. Ask the Spirit of God to use you.

Melt me. Mold me. Fill me. Will you read those words

aloud? Say them slowly and with feeling: *Melt* me. *Mold* me. *Fill* me. *Use* me. Let me press the issue once again: When it comes to relationships, will you ask the Lord to melt you? When it comes to objectives and the pursuit of His will, again I ask, will you say, "Lord, mold me"? And then as the day gets long and the journey gets painful, will you beseech the Lord to fill you? "Fill me with power and perseverance." And as you face the circumstances that are upon you, can you tell the Lord you want Him to transform you? "I want You to be in control, because You're God. I sincerely want You to use me, Lord."

If you meant what you just read—if you are sincerely willing to be reshaped, refreshed, and renewed by the Spirit of God—you will begin to discover a dimension of living you've never known before.

A whole new process will start in your life. And Christ alone will be glorified. In fact, if you really mean business, you will begin living an "unearthly" life . . . nonterrestrial, not mundane.

Some might even call it weird.

Extending Your Roots

1. What does it mean for the Holy Spirit to melt, mold, fill, and use you?

2. The Holy Spirit is a person and wants to heal broken relationships in your life. Think of some barriers that keep you from having a loving, caring relationship with someone.

Decide on the first step you and the Holy Spirit will take to heal your broken relationships.

3. The Holy Spirit comforts us in our sorrows and guides us in our pursuits. He molds us or reshapes us for ministry. For an example of the Holy Spirit active and involved in people's lives, read about the first missionary journey recorded in Acts 13 and 14. Underline in your Bible the involvement of the Holy Spirit in the lives of Barnabas and Paul. What are some definite evidences of molding?

4. The Holy Spirit gives us power and perseverance. He fills us. Read the following verses and discover examples of people who were filled or controlled by the Spirit.
Acts 6:3, 5, 8-10; 7:54-60
Acts 4:8, 31
Acts 6:5; 8:5-13, 35-40
Acts 10:44-45

5. The Holy Spirit transforms our lives. He uses us.
Read Galatians 5:22-23. Describe some practical evidences of a Spirit-filled life.

Taproot

1. The Holy Spirit is active in our salvation. William is a thirty-year-old single, who is not a Christian. Read the suggested Scriptures and note how they speak to Will's situation.

William has been described as the prodigal son before he went back home (Luke 15:11-32). People have prayed for William for years. One day he received word of a special friend's untimely death. William began thinking about himself and even his own sins (John 16:8).

William had reached a turning point. He wanted a different kind of life (John 6:63). People who were praying for William saw their prayers answered. His public profession of faith in Jesus Christ and membership in his local church were evidences of his new life.

William had a growing awareness of the meaning of his salvation (Rom. 8:16). He found new friends, and fellowship with other believers surpassed any of his past relationships (1 Cor.12:13).

William began sharing his new experiences with old friends. He was not afraid to say, "Jesus is my Lord" (v. 3).

The Holy Spirit was real in the life of William.

Provide a conclusion to this story. How can the Holy Spirit melt, mold, fill, and use William?

Notes

Part I: God the Father

Chapter 1

1. Charles W. Colson, *Loving God* (Grand Rapids, Mich.: Zondervan, 1983), 13-14.
2. Charles R. Swindoll, *Improving Your Serve* (Waco, Tex.: Word Books, 1981).
3. Shirley MacLaine, interview, *Washington Post,* 1977.

Chapter 2

1. R. Laird Harris, Gleason L. Archer, Jr., Bruce K. Waltke, *Theological Wordbook of the Old Testament,* (Chicago: Moody Bible Institute, 1980),vol. 2,877.

Chapter 3

1. James M. Boice, *Foundations of the Christian Faith,* vol.1: *The Sovereign God* (Chicago: InterVarsity Press, 1978), 24.

Chapter 6

1. John Powell, *Fully Human, Fully Alive* (Niles, Ill.: Argus Communications, 1976), 17-18.

Chapter 8

1. William Williams, "Guide Me, O Thou Great Jehovah."

Chapter 9

1. J. Robert Raines, *A Creative Brooding* (New York: Macmillan Co., 1977), 345-46.

Part II: The Lord Jesus Christ

Chapter 11

1. Jim Bishop, *The Day Christ Was Born* (New York: Harper & Row, 1961), 16-17.

Chapter 12

1. W. Phillip Keller, *A Layman Looks at the Son of God* (Old Tappan, N.J.: Fleming H. Revell Co., 1977), 56-57.

Chapter 13

1. George MacDonald, quoted in a sermon by J. Vernon McGee entitled "No Room for Him" (Los Angeles: Church of the Open Door, 1967), 7.
2. Leslie Savage, quoted in a sermon by J. Vernon McGee entitled "No Room for Him" (Los Angeles: Church of the Open Door, 1967), 7.

Chapter 15

1. C. S. Lewis, *Mere Christianity* (New York: Macmillan Co., 1970), 40-41.

Chapter 16

1. G. Campbell Morgan, *The Crises of the Christ* (New York: Fleming H. Revell Co., 1936), 79.

Chapter 17

1. © Copyright 1973 by William J. Gaither. Used by permission of Gaither Music Company. From *Alleluia . . . A Praise Gathering for Believers.*
2. Adelaide A. Pollard, "Have Thine Own Way, Lord!"
3. J. Oswald Sanders, *Spiritual Leadership* (Chicago: Moody Press, 1967), 141.

Chapter 18

1. Charles R. Swindoll, *Strengthening Your Grip* (Waco, Tex.: Word Books, 1982), 99-100
2. Clarence E. Macartney, *Of Them He Chose Twelve* (Grand Rapids, Mich.: Baker Book House, 1969), 73-75.

Part III: The Holy Spirit

Chapter 19

1. Billy Graham, *The Holy Spirit* (Waco, Tex.: Word Books, 1978), 24.

Chapter 21

1. Merrill G. Tenney, *John: The Gospel of Belief* (Grand Rapids, Mich.: Wm. B. Eerdmans, 1948), 235.
2. Daniel Iverson, "Spirit of the Living God" (Chicago: Moody Bible Institute, 1963).